ADVANCE PRAISE FOR SCAMMED

Scammed: 3 Steps to Help Your Elder Parents and Yourself *provides a panoramic perspective and simple breakdown of the seemingly endless array of scams that target the elderly with a battle plan to protect and prevent. It will be quite useful and I recommend it!*

~Detective Joe Roubicek, Author of *Financial Abuse of the Elderly; A Detective's Case Files of Exploitation Crimes*
www.exploitationelderly.com

The elderly are easy targets for fraudsters and when scammers strike your own parents, you all suffer. This book will help you protect yourself and your family as well as resolve the conflicts with confidence.

~Mari J. Frank, Esq., author of *The Complete Idiot's Guide to Recovery from Identity Theft and Safeguard Your Identity*

Scammed *is an excellent guide to helping your parent avoid the predators out there. It is easy to understand, practical, evidence-based, thorough, and analytical. A must have.*

~N. Kortner Nygard, Ph.D., Geriatric Psychologist

As a geriatric social worker, I have too often seen the devastating impact of seniors who have been scammed, and I am always looking for tools to protect my seniors. Art's book is very helpful. He skillfully integrates theory with practical advice. This book will greatly benefit professionals who work with seniors, and the adult children of senior parents.

~Warren Lind, M.S.W., L.C.S.W., ASW-G

This is an important book for anyone with elderly parents. It is comprehensive, compassionate, and straightforward in its approach. It can help anyone who is concerned with the safety of their parents and their assets.

~Gregory W. Lester, Ph.D.

D1113049

I have seen firsthand the damage scam artists cause their victims. Unfortunately, it is our elders who are targeted most frequently and suffer the worst consequences. I am so happy Scammed *is available to not only educate the elderly and their loved ones on how to prevent scams, but to help those scammed clean up the destruction left behind. Everyone can benefit from reading* Scammed: 3 Steps to Help Your Elder Parents and Yourself *because education is essential to preventing this form of destruction.*

~Officer Melissa Doss, Community/Media Relations, St. Peters, Missouri, Police Department

Anytime we can help our elderly friends and family remain stable and independent is a beautiful thing. Art Maines teaches us how to help elderly family and friends with a very enjoyable and helpful read. This is a book with valuable skills that we all need to avoid the complex results of the devastation of someone taking advantage of our elderly family and friends.

~Dr. Jim Fogarty, Licensed Clinical Psychologist and national trainer on emotional manipulation.

Scammed *is chock full of useful information and insight that can help you and your parent(s) prevent being scammed and survive the aftermath. In addition to practical steps to aid in prevention and recovery, Art Maines provides a wealth of advice to help heal the emotional and physical aftermath of scams, including a wonderful list of things to say and not say to your folks if it has happened to them.*

~Jennifer L. Abel, Ph.D., author of *Active Relaxation* www.activerelaxationthebook.com

No book has ever tackled the subject of financial predation of the elderly like Scammed. *The book is refreshingly practical and insightful. It's a must-read for anyone dealing with this, either professionally or personally.*

~Steven A. Harvey, MD

Art Maines' book, Scammed: 3 Steps to help your Elder Parents and Yourself *provides a fascinating look at the psychology behind both the victim and the scammer. In addition, the suggestions, advice and assessments are useful for all of us to use with our aging parents. I will now use some of this information to educate and evaluate my elderly mother to insure she does not become a victim.*
~Joanne Waldman, M.Ed., PCC, BCC, LPC, NCC, NCGC, Master Career Counselor, Coach/Director of Training-Retirement Options, New Perspective Coaching

Art Maines skillfully engages the reader with a step by step program to facilitate a financial, physical and emotional recovery plan for seniors who have been scammed. Whether or not a scam has occurred, this is a must read for those who work with seniors or who have an aging parent, as it is the go to guide for protecting our vulnerable seniors from this life changing event. His personal story and examples are poignant reminders that fraud targeting seniors impacts the family system and in turn outlines how to recover from this tragedy together. This book assists the whole family to move from victim to victor in the face of this tragedy. Scammed *will undoubtedly protect and positively affect many lives.*
~ Susan Stevenson Moore, MSW, LCSW
www.FlourishingWell.com

Scammed

3 Steps to Help Your Elder Parents and Yourself

Art Maines, LCSW

Love Your Life

Love Your Life Publishing
St. Peters, MO 63346
www.loveyourlifepublishing.com

ISBN: 978-1-934509-52-4
Library of Congress Control Number: 2012947495
Printed in the United States of America
First Printing 2012
Cover and internal design: Cathy Krebs
Editing by: Gwen Hoffnagle
Author Contact: Art Maines
www.ElderlyFraudRecoveryHelp.com

February, 2014

For Liz + Bill ~

Thanks for attending my talk!

Warmest regards,
Art Maines

DEDICATION

This book is dedicated to my stepfather, Bill, and scam victims and their families everywhere.

ACKNOWLEDGEMENTS

I am deeply grateful to the many people who helped me produce *Scammed*, my first book. I've often read other authors' comments about how creating a book is a collaborative effort, and they are right. I honestly couldn't have done it without all of you!

First, to my wonderful partner, Frank: Thanks for your encouragement and support through the aftermath of Bill's scam victimization, and the ensuing development of this book. I appreciate your patience with all the hours I spent at the computer researching and writing. You're the best!

I further extend my gratitude to the entire Krebs family for their interest in and support of my work, and for the warm inclusion you've all shown me over the years. You guys really are the big family I never had.

A big "thank you" to my deceased mother, Barbara, for always telling me to "go for it." I know if she were here she'd be very proud.

I also want to express appreciation for my chosen family of friends for understanding when I had to stay home and write instead of spending time with you. You know I will do the same for you when the tables are turned.

I'm also very grateful to my colleagues in the fields of social work, psychotherapy, counseling, eldercare, elder law, collections, and publishing who so generously gave of their time to review chapters, offer constructive feedback, and provide me with much-needed guidance. I especially want to recognize Susan Moore, LCSW, Dr. Jennifer Abel, Joe Ilges, Esq., George VonStamwitz, Esq., Alicia VonStamwitz, and Officer Melissa Doss for their generous time and input.

Last but definitely not least, I have to extend huge appreciation to Lynne Klippel of Love Your Life Publishing. You were my dear friend long before this book came to be, and I deeply cherish our friendship. In every sense of the words, I couldn't have done this without you.

Art Maines, LCSW

September, 2012

TABLE OF CONTENTS

FOREWORD

I AM A SCAM VICTIM

I AM A SCAM VICTIM:

I am your mother, father, grandparent, stepparent, neighbor, friend.

I AM A SCAM VICTIM:

I was taken in by one of the nicest people I ever met. He cared about me, asked about my grandchildren, and listened to my stories. I just wanted to help or have a better life when he asked me for money or my credit card number.

I AM A SCAM VICTIM:

When I worked I was a teacher, accountant, lawyer, nuclear sub captain, police officer.

I AM A SCAM VICTIM:

I don't need your blame or judgment; I need your help and support to right the wrong which has been done to me.

I AM A SCAM VICTIM:

I could be you, someday.

INTRODUCTION

Imagine you're cruising along in life, dealing with the ordinary ups and downs. Nothing especially noteworthy is going on, just normal life. Then one day, out of the blue, you are forcefully shoved into a bizarre world which scares the hell out of you. What you face challenges many of your cherished assumptions about life, the people close to you, and even yourself. You feel so much doubt, fear, anger, and sadness coursing through you! Much of what you've learned about the way things are suddenly seems like a shallow, naïve fairy tale. Like most of us who have been there, you've unwillingly entered the world of scams and frauds. Disturbingly, it's an all-too-common part of the seamy underside of growing older today.

When you find out that scam artists have preyed on your elderly parent or other loved one, there's no way to avoid shock and disbelief: "How could this happen?" Then comes the fear—"How much did they get? Do they have access to everything? Is my parent going to be OK?" It's normal for your mind to reel with the frightening possibilities, because they ARE frightening.

This quote from the website www.crimes-of-persuasion.com captures the predicament for fraud victims well:

"Unlike physical abuse, from which a victim can often fully recover once the abuse is put to a stop, financial fraud can result in permanent damage—that is, the loss of the victim's financial independence at a time where he or she has no means of rebuilding a retirement nest egg."

After a lifetime of hard work, saving, and investment, our elders become targets for scammers who are out to impoverish them. It comes at a time in life when our loved ones should be able to relax and enjoy themselves, as well as feel secure about taking care of health problems and end-of-life matters. When you factor in the potential damage to our elders' emotional and physical well-being, this is beyond criminal—in my opinion, it's evil.

Facts and Figures about Fraud against the Elderly

Senior citizens make up about 12 percent (and rising) of the US population, but are approximately 35 percent of all fraud victims. According to the National Consumers League, seniors represent 60 percent of those calling its National Fraud Information Center. Between 2002 and 2003, the 70 to 79 age group rose from 9 percent to 13 percent of all fraud victims, the steepest rise for any age group. The typical victim is female, frail, and mentally impaired. Seventy-five percent are between the ages of 70 and 89.

According to the Ars Technica technology news website, an estimated $41 billion has been lost to date to scammers using the infamous Nigerian or 419 scam. That's $41 billion from just one type of scam. 7.3 million older Americans have been victimized by such scams, according to a new survey. A study by the nonprofit Investor Protection Trust showed that one out of every five Americans over 65 has fallen prey to a financial scam.

Vulnerabilities of Seniors to Frauds

Several factors make seniors more vulnerable to fraud:

- Seniors' desire to help or be charitable opens the door to criminals who tug at their hearts with a phony sob story to rip them off.
- Their generation is typically more trusting of others, which opens opportunities for thieves to abuse that trust.
- Loneliness and social isolation makes a senior more willing to talk with a friendly stranger.
- Seniors are often home when con artists seek their victims.

- Some seniors have lost a degree of physical or mental sharpness, making them even more vulnerable. A few studies even point to changes in elderly peoples' brains that may make them more vulnerable to getting scammed.
- Recent plunges in the stock market and home values have made many seniors much more fearful about their financial situation, opening them up to the all-too-human wish for a fast buck.
- Because people over 50 control 70 percent of the nation's household net worth, they are ripe targets for scammers.
- According to Officer Melissa Doss, when elders get ripped off, it's usually a family member who uncovers the crime. The senior victim is often reluctant to reveal more details because of a fear that their family member will "take over their life" and the senior will no longer be able to live independently. Scammers are very aware of this fear and play on it by telling the victim that their family member is going to prevent them from collecting the big payday. Sometimes the con artist will even tell the senior their family member is out to hurt them. All of this is intended to keep the scam going by cutting off the victim's greatest source of immediate help—those closest to them.

Understanding Scams and Frauds

So what exactly are we talking about here? Scams and frauds (I use the terms interchangeably throughout this book) encompass a vast array of crimes and personal violations that target our loved ones' financial resources and emotional and physical well-being. I use the word *scam* as a synonym for *fraud*, though *scam* sometimes suggests behavior that is deceptive but not necessarily a crime—which fraud is. Both scams and frauds involve the use of trickery or deception for the perpetrator's gain. Fraud includes abuse of the elderly if it occurs in the context of a "relationship in which there is an expectation of trust," as described by the World Health Organization.

There is another important distinction to make between fraud against the elderly and exploitation of the elderly. Exploitation involves using the elderly person's impairments and vulnerability to gain advantage, while fraud implies the victim has the capacity to weigh information and make decisions based on that information. Often this is a distinction without a difference, as a criminal will use exploitation in the commission of what's legally considered a fraud.

Think of it this way:

Scam or fraud = deception of a person with sufficient capacity to make decisions, for the personal gain of the perpetrator.

Exploitation = using a victim's weaknesses or impairments against them.

However we slice it, crimes of this sort cause a lot of damage and pain to our elders; exploitation is particularly heinous.

Parts of a Scam or Fraud

Although every scam is different, they all share certain common features:

- Scouting for potential victims
- Targeting the victim
- Making contact
- Testing for emotional hooks and vulnerabilities, and "grooming" the victim
- Presenting the fraudulent proposal with *emotional activation* and behavioral pressuring
- Obtaining the desired action from the victim
- Repeating the cycle to extend the victimization, or exiting and disappearing

Types of Scams and Frauds

While there are too many types and variations to list, here's a partial list of common frauds and scams affecting elders:

- Advance Fee, Nigerian, or 419 scams: Many people have received this kind through email. In this scam the criminals tell you they have to move some money out of another country (originally Nigeria), and if you help them out you get a percentage of the money. The problem is there is no money, except what THEY take from YOUR bank account. These have been around since at least the '80s. A friend of mine was taken in by one of these in 1988.

- Telemarketing scams: When your parent or other loved one gets ripped off by someone who contacts them over the phone, it's a telemarketing scam.

- Home repair rip-offs: My parents were caught up in one of these a few years ago. An unscrupulous repairman says to the elder, "You need a new_____," and scares them with gory details about what it will cost to do nothing. The problem is, most of the time the elder doesn't have the feared problem at all, or if they do it can be fixed for a fraction of the quoted price.

- Investment scams: A common type is often called the "pump and dump." Crooks buy up a bunch of nearly worthless stock and then pump up the price with bogus reports about how the company is poised to skyrocket in value. When investors buy in, raising the price based on demand, the crooks sell out. The investors get stuck with the loss when the stock plummets back to its original value. Lately there has been a rash of high-pressure investment sales events masquerading as "informational seminars," complete with lunch.

- Magazine subscription "services": These fall into a sort of shadowy, semi-legitimate category. These companies operate in a variety of ways, but all of them are confusing and deceptive. One 79-year-old Caucasian gentleman I knew was getting *Vibe* magazine. Now, it's definitely possible that he had a passion for rap and hip-hop, but when I asked him about it he told me he had no idea why he was receiving that magazine. We discovered he was being billed close to $500 *a month* for a ton of magazines he didn't want.

- Identity theft: Also known as identity fraud, this fraud is particularly upsetting and often hard and time-consuming to handle. I've devoted a whole chapter to this problem because it's still the #1 fraud in the country.

- Phony sweepstakes and lotteries: The Canadian Lottery scam has cost hundreds of people thousands of dollars. The problem is it's against federal law for a US citizen to participate in a foreign lottery.

- Caregiver fraud: Sometimes "trusted" caregivers use their relationships with our parents and their access to private information for their own enrichment. Ed Carnot, Esq., tells a heart-wrenching story about his dad getting ripped off by someone he trusted in his book *Is Your Parent in Good Hands?*

- Relationship-based, Romeo Rip-off, or Sweetheart scams: This is when someone gets taken by a good-looking younger person who seems genuinely interested in them. Usually it's a handsome man who romances a lonely, elderly woman. He skips out once he's drained her for as much money as he can get.

- The Grandchild Stuck in a Foreign Country ruse: The crooks call Grandma or Grandpa, claiming to be their grandchild who's stuck in a foreign country and needs money to get out of a jam, usually jail. The frightened, unwitting elder wires the money out of the country, where it cannot be recovered. 7.3 million older Americans have been victimized by such scams, according to a recent survey.

- A different, hybrid version of a relationship-based scam in which a family member is the perpetrator: A combination of a relationship-based scam plus financial abuse of the elderly, these are very painful, divisive, and damaging to a family, and often wrenchingly difficult to resolve well.

As you can see, there seems to be no end to the scammers' creativity in developing new ways to victimize our parents (and us!).

My main purpose in writing this book is to help you help your parent or other loved one deal with and recover from the awful experience of getting ripped off by professional scam artists. I provide the three steps I took in handling a series of scams perpetrated on my 82-year-old stepfather in 2009. Though the specific details of your experience will be different from mine, I provide ideas and resources to help you manage and minimize the damage from this type of crime. At times you will need to be creative and flexible in how you apply the steps and the order in which you carry them out; there's no substitute for common sense.

Another reason I wrote *Scammed* is to add to the discussion about how we can more effectively help elders stay safe from scammers. I frequently give talks and presentations on scam and fraud prevention to elder organizations and professional groups, and I've found them receptive and eager to learn. I'm convinced we can do better at teaching our seniors how to spot likely frauds and steer clear of them.

How *Scammed* Can Help You

In Section One, I introduce you to my stepfather, Bill, and tell his story in more depth. I intend that reading the story of his victimization will help you realize that fraud happens to really good, intelligent people. Some folks have the idea that people who are hurt by con artists are stupid, naïve, or somehow deserved it. Nothing could be further from the truth.

The first three chapters lay out ideas and suggested resources for navigating what I've come to think of as the three steps of handling a scammed parent. I wish I could tell you exactly how to deal with your particular situation, but the three steps, with the right modifications, apply to the majority of cases. I'll say this repeatedly throughout the book: Get good professional help from lawyers, financial advisors, counselors, physicians, and others, using my steps as a starting point.

Section Two deals with the emotional aspects of fraud recovery, both for your parent and for you as their helper and caregiver. Elder victimization of this sort is an ugly experience. Many elders are already living financially close to the bone, especially with the recent stock market and home price declines. Getting scammed is a form of personal violation that leaves wounds and fears that often don't go away quickly or easily. I talk about the emotional effects on seniors from getting taken, and how to help them, in Chapter 4.

You may have thought (like me), "It can't happen to me (or my parent)," but statistics prove otherwise. If you have elderly parents or relatives, scammers ARE targeting them. It's frightening, and it's happening more all the time. I tell my clients that having information and a plan relieves anxiety, so I hope you find the information in this book helpful and as comforting as possible under the circumstances. Chapter 5 addresses the necessity to take good care of yourself during the ordeal of helping your elderly parent handle things and recover.

In Chapter 6 I tackle the psychology of scamming from both sides of the issue, the victim's and the perpetrator's. I talk about how criminals use various techniques to get to our parents and other loved ones. I draw from my work as a psychotherapist and counselor and my familiarity with certain forms of psychological dysfunction called personality disorders to cast some light on what's likely going on with the criminals.

Some authorities and writers say scams and frauds can never be fully prevented. They may be right. Nevertheless, I'm convinced that understanding some basics of the psychology of scamming and victimization can be helpful in prevention. In Section Three I offer three chapters with my ideas for more effectively preventing scams and fraud.

Chapters 10, 11, and 12 are where I put the steps in practice to help you deal with three common scams affecting elders. These are telemarketing, home repair, and identity theft. I go over some important differences in how to handle the recovery phase for each one, and I provide checklists and resources to guide you on your way.

The appendix is your comprehensive resource guide, listing a wealth of resources including books, websites, and organizations I've found helpful. There's a surprising amount of help available out there for you and your loved one—if you know where to look.

In my day job, I am a licensed mental health professional (licensed clinical social worker) actively providing counseling and psychotherapy to a full practice of clients. After I saw (and experienced) what happened to my stepfather, I realized I had a chance to help more people in a different way by sharing what I've learned, and researched the field of fraud against the elderly. I hope you find this book and its companion website and blog, www.elderlyfraudrecoveryhelp.com, helpful. I encourage you to share your story and any other useful resources you are aware of with me and others (with your permission, of course) through this website.

Keep in mind that I AM NOT a lawyer or certified financial planner. Please consult with the appropriate professionals for your situation, as this book is not intended to replace advice from qualified experts. All information was current as of the writing of this book. I use the terms "parent" and "child" for easy understanding, but the ideas obviously apply to any similar situation.

Best of luck, and let me know if I can help you and your parent in some way. Always remember you're not alone.

SECTION ONE

Getting Scammed and the Recovery Steps

Bill's Story

I was about six years old when I first met my stepfather. My parents' marriage had ended because of my father's drinking problem, and I had no idea at the time who this stranger would become in my life. He seemed nice enough, and my house became much quieter without the constant fighting. He was fine with me!

Over the years, Bill and I became very good friends. He took me to fly kites and do dad stuff. He and my mom got along well for the most part, so life settled into a kind of routine. He taught me to drive when I got to the teen years, and I came to realize I could count on him if I needed him.

After my mom and Bill retired, they began to travel. My mother was especially fond of cruises, having grown up on the coast of Maine. Bill grew up on the plains of Oklahoma, but he seemed to enjoy being on the ocean as well. I think it was primarily that he enjoyed being with my mother, whom he adored.

As my mother's health began to decline in the '90s, Bill and I became a stronger team for her care. A lifetime of smoking, stress, and overwork took its toll on Mom, and she finally had to breathe oxygen full time. Bill cheerfully handled every new challenge thrown our way as her health deteriorated, even as he had to do more and more for her. I was living 1,200 miles away in Missouri, while they continued to live in my hometown in South Texas. Nevertheless, if either or both of them needed me, I was on the next plane out.

In May of 2005 the three of us were planning to go on a cruise for Mom's 77th birthday. She had just gotten the green light from her long-time physician to take the trip, so we took off for Fort Lauderdale. I've often thought that she knew something was wrong, but we went anyway.

She held both of our hands on the descent into Florida, which was unusual. As we touched down, I started to realize things were not going well for her. She never complained, but she grew more and more unresponsive, finally slumping forward in her wheelchair on the jetway.

What followed was a blur. The airline crew called the paramedics, who worked to resuscitate her on the spot. I stayed with her while Bill went to alert the cruise line representative who was meeting our flight. Mom regained consciousness and was taken to a nearby hospital.

Bill and I had been a team for years regarding her care, but now we stood by as the doctors tried to save her. We supported each other over the next 12 hours as she slipped further and further away. She died early the next morning.

So here we were in Florida on what was supposed to be a vacation, but now we were facing the unimaginable. We went to work, arranging the myriad details for the funeral and our own transportation. Bill had to go back to Texas, and I had to go back to Missouri, before we went to Maine, where my mother had requested that the funeral and burial be held.

After the funeral Bill and I had a discussion about his future and options. He, like me, is an only child, so I am his only family. He was 75 at the time of my mother's passing, so I knew he would likely need someone to help him out as his needs for care increased. I proposed that he move to Missouri so my partner and I could look after him, and he agreed. He arrived in St. Louis in November of 2005.

Perhaps it was the stress of losing his partner of 38 years, or maybe it was just the seemingly inevitable problems that come with aging, but Bill began 2006 with a string of health problems that pushed both of us to our limits. First came a broken hip while he was in Texas handling some estate-related matters. Then came a terrible case of shingles on his head and face, causing excruciating pain for months. Finally, in November of 2006, Bill's kidneys failed and he needed permanent dialysis three days a week.

We worked through all of that and settled into a new routine. Bill's quality of life seemed quite good for the most part. We got together often, and he began attending our church for its loving and inclusive community. He was warmly welcomed into my partner's large family, always being invited for holidays and other celebrations. He never complained about money or financial worries. My mother's ambition and hard work had helped leave him reasonably secure.

As I look back on the story I can now see that there were some important warning signs that Bill was vulnerable to fraud. In the late '90s, during one of the many hospital stays my mother endured, a traveling handyman came to the door and said their house had some cracks in the brick exterior that required urgent attention. This became a larger job with the handyman's diagnosis of a serious problem with the sewer line from their house out to the main line. Bill, not wanting to upset my mom further with this issue, told the guy to do whatever he needed to fix the problems.

It turned out that the "handyman" was a scam artist preying on the elderly in the area. The problems he identified were enormously overblown, and what should have been about a $10,000 job for the sewer line became a $60,000 debacle. I called in a consulting engineer to take a look at the mess. He told me that scammers were rampant in that area of South Texas and the laws were such that if they were shut down they would just file bankruptcy and set up shop under a new name.

Scammed

Despite the problem with the fraudulent house repairs in the '90s, I was shocked by the magnitude of the 2009 scam against Bill. He called me in mid-May asking for help with wiring money. I had spoken to him about never sending money to people who said he had won a prize, thinking I was being proactive about looking after him. I asked him what was going on, and he told me some people had told him he had won a prize in a sweepstakes but they needed money from him for "taxes, processing fees, and customs." I smelled a rat right away and told him not to send any money. He admitted he had already sent about $1,600, but said he wouldn't send any more. In short, I thought I was doing everything right.

That little fantasy came crashing down on June 12, 2009. My partner and I were in Wisconsin for a friend's ordination celebration. I listened dumbstruck as a detective from the town where Bill lived told me over the phone how employees of the local grocery store had captured an image of him from the store's security camera and used it to alert her that Bill was being ripped off. They had observed a pattern of his wiring money abroad. They had entered his name and picture on the store's alert sheet which directed employees on all shifts to refuse to wire any more money for him.

The detective went on to describe how she and a uniformed police officer had confronted Bill in the store. I couldn't believe it as she told me how he had "gone off on them," using language I had never heard Bill use, ever. I remember asking the detective, "You're talking about Bill _____?" I couldn't believe this was happening. It didn't sound like the Bill I had known for most of my life.

The detective finished her story about the extent of the crime against Bill ($30,000 in total losses was her estimate at the time). She had solid evidence that he had been using credit card cash advances to wire money from multiple locations since early February. Curiously,

I felt myself growing calmer and going into my crisis mode. I have an ability to get very calm when things get stirred up, and I go into problem-solving mode pretty quickly. A plan for handling this mess came together in my mind, step by step; I knew what I had to do.

I got on the phone immediately, calling all the financial institutions I knew bill had accounts with. My goal was to get as much information as I could from the detective and others, and then stop the bleeding and lock down Bill's assets to prevent further victimization. I also called Sara, our trusted friend who visited Bill once a week to provide companionship and help him with household chores. I asked her to get Bill's credit cards from him since he had used them to get the cash advances he had sent to the crooks. All of this took a surprisingly short time—a couple of hours at most. I knew the next step was to call Bill myself and confront him. I couldn't afford to wait until I flew back to Missouri.

I wish I could say my calmness continued into that phone call, but by now my anger was rising in a big way. I had worked so hard to protect him and look after him, and the impossible had happened. I was livid.

I firmly believe that I have to practice what I preach to my clients. If I can't or won't do something, how can I expect the people who come to me for therapy to do it? So I took a little time to think about what was coming next and how I was feeling, trying to settle myself and prepare for what I had to say. I'm glad I did that, because when I called him, though I unleashed my anger and frustration in ways that I hoped expressed my outrage with the situation and anger and frustration with him, I was able to avoid damaging the relationship. I knew I was the only person he had to help, and I truly didn't want him to be hurt further. Besides, it wasn't about me; it was about Bill and his future.

Scammed

I told him what I had heard from the detective, and he confirmed that the confrontation had happened. I let him know how angry I was that he hadn't listened to me when I had warned him about scams like this, and hadn't checked with me before sending money to anyone he didn't know. I went on about how he had lied to me when he said in May that he wasn't going to send more money to the criminals, since the detective had verified that he had wired several thousand dollars more since then. I also told him Sara was on her way to his house that evening to collect his credit cards and hold them for me until I returned, and I asked him for his cooperation with this plan. He listened without getting overly defensive, and agreed to give the credit cards (*"ALL OF THEM!"* I said) to Sara. What scared me was his continuing belief that the scammers were his friends and that he would get a big check the following Monday.

When I returned home I went straight to Bill's condo. We talked for some time about the details of the scam, such as what he knew about the people he had been wiring money to. While I was there he received a phone call from one of the scammers which revealed that Bill's home phone number hadn't been successfully changed yet. He mentioned again his conviction that I was wrong and he was going to get a big check the next day.

The next day he showed me large piles of receipts from the money wiring and an astounding number of names and phone numbers for the scammers. We made arrangements to meet with the detective in two days to file a police report. This was Monday evening, the day he was supposed to get the big check. By now he had figured out that he wasn't getting the money, because he apologized to me for causing all the trouble and said he knew he had made a giant mistake. He promised he would cooperate with everything we needed to do. I thanked him for that and apologized for any overly harsh words or tone in our conversation right after the discovery of the scam.

The meeting with the detective was enlightening and sobering. Bill was highly apologetic for his behavior in the grocery store on the day she and the other officer had confronted him, and she accepted graciously. She explained that there was almost no chance of recovering any of his money since he wired it overseas, and that the US Secret Service has jurisdiction over crimes such as this. She talked about how common scams and frauds against the elderly are. She took all of Bill's original receipts and papers to use in filing the police report, and said she would pass them on to a contact she had at the Secret Service. Our best hope would be to help others avoid being ripped off by helping the federal law enforcement officials. We agreed, and she said she would return copies of everything to us along with the police report.

I spent virtually every spare moment for the next three months working on what I call Step 3, the recovery plan. This meant numerous calls to credit card fraud investigators, trying to find a decent attorney, and assessing the true magnitude of the crimes against Bill. I was blown away when the detective came back with a final figure of $70,000 in total losses!

Unfortunately, most of the credit card company employees weren't particularly helpful. They expressed their concern, and occasionally offered some great advice off the record. The problem was that the crimes were against Bill, not the banks. The criminals had effectively cut Bill off from the fraud protections banks have in place for their customers by having him take cash advances. We would have to figure this out on our own.

I initially met with a bankruptcy attorney recommended by our elder law attorney. She said she had met him at a law conference, and then confessed he was the only one she knew. The bankruptcy attorney told me that Bill wasn't a candidate for bankruptcy because he had too many assets, but seemed to have no clue about how to craft a reasonable plan for addressing the problems without leaving Bill dangerously low on money for his potential end-of-life care. We decided to move on to another attorney.

The new attorney, Dave, seemed to "get it" right away. He listened as Bill and I told the story, only asking questions as necessary for clarification. As a counselor and therapist, I size up other professionals by their listening skills, and Dave passed the test.

He began laying out his ideas about how we could proceed. I had come up with some ideas before the meeting, which I had discussed thoroughly with Bill. Dave told us, in no uncertain terms, that our options were very limited. He did think, however, there was a good chance for Bill to emerge from this without more serious damage. He agreed we needed to do everything possible to preserve as many of Bill's modest assets as possible to provide for his potential end-of-life care.

Since that time we have continued to work the plan through numerous ups and downs. Through it all, Dave has been a guiding and comforting presence. This is why I believe that getting a good lawyer to help with all you're dealing with is essential.

Bill has proven remarkably resilient through his ordeal. Our parents are often tougher than we think. He's had his time of regret and guilt, and I've certainly had to work through my own anger, guilt, and fear. We are far from the final outcome of all of this, but I am more convinced than ever that with the right information, resources, and a willingness to persevere and be flexible, you and your parent can get through it, too.

Chapter 1

Step 1—Discovery: Gather the Vital Information Quickly

"Not having the information you need when you need it leaves you wanting. Not knowing where to look for that information leaves you powerless."
—Author Lois Horowitz

This is the "Oh my God" phase. No matter how you find out about the scam, you will go through a flood of emotions, especially anger and fear. At first you won't believe this is happening to your parent and you. I say "you," because if you're reading this you are probably either totally or partially responsible for cleaning up the mess. And trust me, it IS a mess.

I was out of town when I got the call from the detective. My first reaction was intense fear, thinking Bill was dead or injured. What the detective said stunned me. She had been gathering information for weeks attempting to shut down the scam. I'll never forget seeing the grainy image of my stepfather standing at the store's courtesy desk as he waited to wire his life savings to criminals.

If You Think Your Parent Might Be Getting Scammed, But You're Not Quite Sure

A vital part of the discovery step is to determine as accurately as you can that there is, in fact, a scam going on. A common question

I get from people who email me is how to tell when a parent is getting scammed. I encourage them to trust their instincts about it, and follow that up with checking things out. Sometimes you're not sure, but things feel "off" in some way. The key here is to look for *something different* in your parent's transactions or patterns—something that indicates the presence of a crime. It's not about being suspicious or paranoid; it's about positive vigilance and paying attention.

Learn from my mistake. Bill asked me for help with wiring money to someone about a month before the scam fully came to light. This was the first indication that he had fallen under the scammers' spell. Naturally I saw the warning sign and told him to immediately stop sending money. He had already sent $1,600, and couldn't stop that, but I told him not to send any more. I thought, "Well, $1,600 is bad, but it could have been a whole lot worse." I thought the nightmare was over. What I didn't do was follow up with him and check on whether he was still in contact with the crooks and subject to their *deceptulation*—a word I coined to describe the combination of the deception and manipulation that are at the core of the scammers' tricks. (For more about deceptulation, see Chapter 6.) In the final month of the scam he wired over $15,000!

So what signs should you look for that indicate a scam is likely occurring? In my work with clients I talk a lot about "red lights on your dashboard." These are the signs of a problem which we ignore at our peril. Just as you wouldn't ignore a big, ugly, red light on your dashboard telling you "CHECK BRAKES," don't ignore the following warning signs:

Red Lights on Your Dashboard for Possible Fraud

- Sudden changes in your parent's bank accounts or banking behaviors, especially unexplained withdrawals of large sums of money

- Unexplained or unplanned changes in your parent's investment accounts
- The appearance of magazines that don't fit your parent's usual interests
- A lot of what I call "useless crap" around your parent's house. Sometimes questionable organizations send small trinkets like pens, calendars, etc. to create the illusion of providing value and keep people sending money.
- Unauthorized withdrawal of your parent's funds via their ATM card—particularly repeated withdrawals over a short period of time
- Your parent tells you they won a sweepstakes, lottery, or prize.
- Services or home repairs that are not necessary, or which seem unusually expensive
- The sudden appearance of credit card balances, especially for cash advances, with no prior history of using credit.
- Your parent's description of money being tight, or a sudden reluctance to spend money for reasonable expenses that were never an issue before
- Your parent seems evasive when you ask about money.
- You hear names of new "friends" who don't fit your parent's usual interactions.
- You discover that significant property is missing.

Getting Started

So what is your goal for this step? *Get as much information as you can, as quickly as you can.* You have to figure out what happened in order to know how to stop the bleeding and lock down your parent's assets in Step 2. Elders who have been taken by scammers often go through a lot of shame, embarrassment, and denial, so your mom or dad may not tell you everything. (Bill still believed he was going to get a big check as late as three days after the scam was exposed.) They may also have thinking or memory impairments that block your ability to figure out all that's happened. A 2008 Duke University study showed that 35 percent of people over age 71 in the US have either mild cognitive impairment or Alzheimer's disease—that's 9 million people.

Here's how to start: Ask *everyone* you can *everything* you can, beginning with the two most important questions for your parent:

- "Has anyone threatened to hurt you or someone close to you if you don't do what they demand?" (If so, notify law enforcement about this IMMEDIATELY if they aren't already involved. Clearly this is a potential safety threat.)
- "Did you give the people you talked to any account numbers, passwords, your Social Security number, or any other unique or security-related information?" (If they have, it's an even worse EMERGENCY and requires ACTION NOW; your mom or dad may also be a victim of identity theft. Go directly to the action steps in Step 2 (Chapter 2) for locking down your parent's assets and stopping any further losses. And see Chapter 12 on recovering from identity theft.)

Here are a few more important questions to ask:

- How much money (approximately)?
- How often? Has this happened more than once?
- To whom was the money sent or given?
- Did you ever receive money and send it on to another person?
- Which account(s) are involved?
- How was the money accessed? By whom?
- Can you show me any receipts, phone records, or other papers pertaining to what's happened?

Start collecting every bit of evidence you can grab. It may not help you get any of your parent's money back, but may prove useful later. The police will need all available evidence to write their report, and you'll need that report to talk to financial institutions about settlements or other forms of relief that may be available.

Watch for Multiple Forms of Victimization

Another painful part of being hurt in a scam or fraud is the potential for multiple kinds of victimization. It's quite common for criminals to try to extract money and personal information in many different ways at the same time. Because of this, it's vital to be thorough in gathering information in order to catch other forms of fraud that could be co-occurring with the first one you discover.

The Legal Tool You Need to Help Your Parent

You will need a legal document called a *power of attorney* to gain access to information about your parent's accounts from the institutions. Many employees at financial institutions won't even talk to you without receiving a power of attorney first, although I had no trouble getting people at Bill's financial institutions to temporarily freeze his accounts. I simply told them Bill had been the victim of a scam and they were eager to help. Some of them even told me how frequently things like this happen.

A power of attorney is for your parent's protection, since anyone can say they are your parent's child and cause problems. It's a good idea to have a power of attorney drawn up by an elder law attorney in your area well before something happens, but you can often get it done quickly in an emergency. Remember that I am not an attorney and this book is not intended to replace advice from a qualified elder law attorney. Please check the National Academy of Elder Law Attorneys at http://www.naela.org for the name of a qualified attorney in your area. You might also ask trusted professionals, friends, family, or colleagues for referrals. If your parent or other family members are concerned about your having too much influence, remember that powers of attorney can be revoked at any time, such as when the crisis has passed.

Finding a good attorney can be hard. The first one I consulted about the situation didn't work out, and I've seen a number of my clients struggle with poor lawyers. Here are a few ideas about selecting a good one based on the word LAWYER:

L = **L**istens

A = **A**nswers your questions

W = **W**illing to work with you

Y = **Y**our parent's needs are their first priority

E = **E**ncourages you and expects to find a reasonable, positive way out of the mess

R = **R**eturns your phone calls promptly

Your attorney is likely to be the first member of your recovery team—the professionals and other trusted people you call on for their expertise and help with scam recovery. In the steps that follow you will continue to add more people to your recovery team as appropriate for your parent's situation.

Emotional Issues for Seniors in Step 1

It's important to remember that your parent will be in shock and denial, or at least be very upset. Such emotions are not helpful in this situation, but don't badger or pressure your parent. If they seem to need a break, let them take one. Signs of needing a break include:

- Increasing agitation or crabbiness
- Crying or other signs of sadness
- A kind of spacey, distracted quality in their speech and/or manner
- Worsening of physical or mental health symptoms—for example, they seem more anxious
- Outright refusal to discuss the matter

You know your parent and how they react to stress and upsets. If you think they're getting upset, trust that. I describe the emotional toll on seniors in greater detail in Chapter 4. For now, expect a lot of "I don't know" answers, because the scammers want to make things as complicated as possible to confuse your parent and keep the crime going.

If your mom or dad has normal age-related memory slippage or a touch of dementia, they may not know all of what's happening to them. See if you can get the information you need to protect them from another source, or do what you can do for the moment without causing them further distress, and accept that it may not be perfect. The crimes against Bill came to light in layers over several days. It's easy to get caught up in the urgency of the situation, but keep in mind that your parent is more important than the money!

Ask for Help from Trusted People, and Be a Detective

Remember to ask your other parent, siblings, friends, and other family members *you trust* for their ideas without revealing anything too sensitive. If you're not sure you trust them, it's probably better to choose someone else to speak with. Your emotions will be running wild during this time, and as I tell my clients, "When we stress, we regress," meaning you may not be thinking as clearly as usual because of the stress you're under. This is a time to draw on your circle of trusted advisors. Words you may find useful are: "I have good reason to suspect Mom/Dad has been the target of scammers. I don't know how bad it is yet, but I could use your help to protect them. I've asked these questions: _____. Can you think of anything I've forgotten to ask?"

You will probably have to do some detective work, too. Your parent may be too upset or agitated to be of much help. Sometimes parents are actually angry at their child for interrupting their hoped-for big payday! Go through your parent's bank statements or go online and see if you can find more evidence of unexplained withdrawals (of course, ask for permission first if you can). Ask questions from multiple angles and in different ways.

Look for stacks of paperwork and phone numbers. Many older people keep everything they've been using close at hand because they long longer get around as easily as they used to. Does your parent keep everything on a TV tray or in some other highly stacked location? That's where you look. I found dozens of receipts for wire transfers on a table close to Bill's favorite chair. You may also find bank, brokerage, and credit card statements with the phone numbers you'll need in Step 2.

So what do I mean by "get the vital information *quickly?*" Get the first two crucial questions discussed in "Getting Started" above ("Has anyone threatened to hurt you or someone close to you if you don't do what they demand? Did you give the people you talked to any account numbers, passwords, your Social Security number, or any other unique or security-related information?") answered immediately—within minutes of discovering the fraud. Safety is the first priority, and you must move fast if your dad or mom has given the crooks personal information. Identity thieves have been known to create and use a copy of a victim's credit or debit card halfway around the world *within 30 minutes!* Police say the first 48 hours after a crime are crucial, but that may be too long for many frauds and scams.

If you aren't sure how bad things are, assume the worst at this stage. Always err on the side of caution, especially in Step 1. Think like a scammer—where else would you find money to take from your parent? Remember, your goal for this step is to get as much information about the scam and how it was carried out as you can, and to discover all the avenues to your parent's resources the crooks may have used. Check on the whereabouts of things like car titles, jewelry, and even the deed to the house. Keep in mind that the crooks are probably using your parent's personal information to perpetrate identity theft, too.

I recommend you refer to the apparent criminals as "the people you spoke to" and use similar non-judgmental language when speaking with your parent. The reason for this is strategic; you want to gain your parent's cooperation in Step 1. They may not yet realize that their "friend" who was "so nice" is, in fact, a ruthless crook bent on ripping them off.

Keep Good Records

Remember to document everything! Being organized with all the information you gather is a must, not just in Step 1 but throughout the aftermath of your parent's victimization. Depending on the type of fraud or scam, you may need the information for law enforcement personnel or attorneys. You will also be interacting with all kinds of institutions and people, many friendly to your cause, some indifferent or even hostile. If you have your act together it makes you more confident, therefore you seem more professional. This, in turn, may make it more likely that the employees and organizations you work with will take you seriously. I suggest the following ideas for organizing the information pertinent to your parent's situation:

Notebook for a phone log:

Write down the names and titles of the people you speak with, their phone and fax numbers (direct phone number if you can get it), postal and email addresses, plus dates and times of calls.

Filing system:

You need to have a system for storing paper and electronic documents so you have easy access to them later. Set up file

19

folders in a separate, locking file box for scam-related papers. Create a filing system on your computer for emails and electronic documents, and make sure the information is password-protected and that you back it up regularly—at least weekly.

Master log book:

It's important to keep track of lots of details as you help your parent recover. Here are some basics to put in your master log book:

- Names/phone numbers/email addresses
- Institutions/companies/agencies
- How you contacted people (phone, email, fax, letter, etc.)
- Date and time of all contacts
- Planned date and time for follow-up
- A brief summary (just a few words) of what happened or was said during the contact
- Scam-related expenses

Crime Timeline

You might need to hire an attorney or even go to court over your parent's fraud victimization, and having a *crime timeline* will help you remember details. Memory is notoriously unreliable, and if your parent has some memory loss, a crime timeline could be invaluable. Record every event as best you can, by date, with a brief summary of what happened. Start with either your parent's initial story of what happened or what you remember as you detected the scam, and keep it current as you work through Steps 2 and 3. Don't get hung up on trying to remember everything precisely; just do your best.

Additional benefits of keeping good records are that your parent may be able to deduct their scam-related losses and recovery expenses on their taxes, and if the scammer is caught it may help in collecting restitution. You'll read more about this in the three chapters on recovery from individual types of scams in Section Four.

To further help you with organizing your efforts, in Section Four I've included checklists of questions to ask and tasks to accomplish in each step. These will help you organize your thoughts and respond more effectively. They will also help when it comes time to file a police report and deal with the different types of institutions you'll be encountering in Steps 2 and 3.

Remember that it's OK to ask for help. If you aren't good at organization, get help from someone you trust who *is* good at it. Don't let yourself get overwhelmed, and take frequent breaks to clear your head.

When a Bad Situation Is Even Worse: A Family Member or Caregiver is Ripping Off Your Parent

The unfortunate truth is that all too often the person ripping off your parent is your sibling or one of your parents' grandchildren. Caregivers also rip off the people they are supposed to be looking after. Such acts are what Detective Joe Roubicek calls *exploitation crimes* in his book *Financial Abuse of the Elderly: A Detective's Case Files of Exploitation Crimes.* Exploitation is when someone uses the victim's impairment(s) to gain an advantage over them, usually to steal from them. Exploitation crimes typically fall under the legal definition of *financial abuse.*

No one likes to think about someone they know exploiting a loved one, but the emails and stories I receive show just how disturbingly common this is. Love of money really seems to be the root of all evil, especially in this situation. Add to this other evils like addiction, desperation, and entitlement thinking ("I deserve some of Grandma's money") that may be motivating the perpetrator, and the stage is set for some incredibly painful family problems.

Here are some signs of possible financial abuse:

- A caregiver or family member doesn't allow you to see your parent by themselves.
- Your parent isn't dressing appropriately, or their hygiene practices seem to be diminishing even though a caregiver is present.
- You hear names of new "friends" who don't fit your parent's usual interactions.
- You discover significant property is missing.
- Your parent tells you they are being financially exploited (rare, but it happens).
- The recent addition of authorized signers on your parent's bank signature card
- Unauthorized withdrawal of your parent's funds via their ATM card—particularly repeated withdrawals over a short period of time
- Sudden changes in bank accounts or banking behaviors, especially unexplained withdrawal(s) of large sums of money
- Unexplained or unplanned changes in investment accounts
- The sudden appearance of credit card balances, especially for cash advances, with no prior history of using credit.
- Excessive or unusual cash-back transactions at the grocery store, pharmacy, etc.
- Your parent's description of money being tight, or other indications of sudden reluctance to spend money for reasonable expenses that were never an issue before.

Discovery in the Case of Financial Abuse

So what can you do about this? Be prepared to make some hard choices and endure family ugliness. You'll have to do your homework to get the proof you'll need to allege undue influence and challenge legal documents the perpetrator may have manipulated your loved one into signing. You will likely need good legal advice and help. Even then, sadly, you may not prevail.

Gather evidence to establish a paper trail for the financial abuse. You will probably need a power of attorney to make much headway with this, although I've found that people want to help when you tell them what's going on. Follow the record-keeping recommendations from earlier in this chapter and create an account of your allegations against the person.

Gather your information in secret to the extent possible. Tipping off your exploitative family member or caregiver will only cause them to go deeper under cover or take other steps to protect their plan.

What are you looking for? Here's a partial list:

- Legal documents related to the abuse
- Dates and details of significant medical diagnoses, especially for disorders that would impair your parent's reasoning and judgment, such as Alzheimer's disease. If you don't already have one, get your parent to sign a Health Insurance Portability and Accountability Act (HIPAA) release so you can talk to their doctor(s) about their medical conditions. Your legal options are probably limited unless your parent has such a diagnosis. The law only considers physical harm to oneself, not financial harm, when assessing legal competence. Without a HIPAA release, you have to work harder and more behind the scenes to handle such a situation.
- Medical records showing dates and results of mental status exams, if your parent has taken any.
- Receipts, bank statements, investment account statements, credit card statements, etc. for all questionable financial transactions and account changes.

Think about others in your family. Is there anyone you can trust fully who may be as concerned as you are about your parent's well-being? Have a discreet conversation with them about what you've discovered and, perhaps, whether they're willing to help you in some way.

Speak with your local Adult Protective Services workers, an experienced and responsive elder law attorney, and, if possible, a police detective knowledgeable about financial abuse of the elderly. It's important to research the legal options in your state. If any of your first contacts seem less than interested or helpful, ask to talk to someone else.

Dealing with situations like this is grueling. Make sure you have at least one person you can comfortably talk to about it. Prepare to be shocked, disgusted, and furious when you learn the full extent of what's happened.

Again, I can't hope to provide all the questions you will need to ask. I hope this chapter will at least help you get started and be ready to move into Step 2.

Chapter 2

Step 2—Protect Your Parent: Stop the Bleeding and Lock Down Their Assets

"The best lightning rod for your protection is your own spine."
—Ralph Waldo Emerson

In Step 2, it's about *stopping the bleeding* and *locking down the assets*. The crooks are like locusts—they will strip your parent of every asset they can get to. They might have your parent sell everything or take out huge credit card debt by coaching them to use cash advances. People have taken out second mortgages on paid-for houses to fund such crimes. This is why it's so important to gather all the information you can in Step 1 so you know exactly what to do to stop this thing in its tracks NOW.

Step 2 fundamentally requires taking effective action to protect your parent. It's the meat of handling a scam or fraud. Get this part right, and you can rest somewhat in the comfort of knowing that your dad or mom isn't in any further immediate danger.

Because of your hard work in Step 1, you should know enough at this point to begin protecting your parent. Nevertheless, keep asking questions as they come up. Now is the time to TAKE ACTION.

What to Do if Your Parent Doesn't "Get It": The Problem of Denial and Hiding

Scammers are unbelievably skillful at creating a kind of brainwashing in elders – getting our parents to think they are totally legitimate, even nice people. Criminals do this through the clever use of psychological principles and practices (more about this in Chapter 6). Add to this the shame that victims of these crimes feel, and you get parents who either pretend everything is OK while the scammers are siphoning off their life savings, or truly don't understand what's happening. This makes your task harder and requires you to take specific actions.

Naturally we want to respect our parents' independence and autonomy. But one of the more bizarre and troubling parts of handling fraud against them is the way the crooks get our parents to believe *we* are the problem. Therefore, I argue for the necessity of "borrowing" your parent's free will for the briefest time possible in order to protect them from the crooks and themselves, most typically through a power of attorney. This may turn into a longer or permanent arrangement depending on your parent's impairments, but it's a crucial first step. I've heard from people who know their mom or dad is getting ripped off, but are fearful of taking action to sever the contact between their parent and the criminals because they don't want to compromise their parent's autonomy. My position is this: The priority is to take action to *protect* your parent.

Is Your Parent in Denial? Consider an Intervention

You may be familiar with the idea of an intervention from the TV show of the same name, or from hearing or reading about it. Interventions are usually associated with addiction, but they apply to denial regarding scam and fraud crimes as well. An intervention means doing as much as you can to help your parent see the light and hear the plain truth about what's happening from people they trust and respect.

You may need to conduct a kind of intervention with a parent who is under a criminal's spell. The criminals deviously get your parent to believe their lies so they can rip them off. It's up to you and your family, friends, and other members of your care team and recovery team to help them shake off the power of the scammers' lies. You have to sever the contact between your parent and the person(s) victimizing them if you can. If your parent continues to have contact with the criminal, they will still be under their influence. For my Guide to Scam Denial Interventions, please go to my website, www. elderlyfraudrecoveryhelp.com, and download this guide.

Build a Financial Firewall

If you haven't already done this in Step 1, now is the time to call your parent's bank, credit union, broker, credit card issuers, and any other financial institutions involved. Identify yourself and tell them what's happened. Ask them to freeze the accounts or place a fraud alert on them.

Next, call the three credit reporting agencies, Experian, Trans Union, and Equifax (see the resources in the appendix for the phone numbers), and have them place a fraud alert on your parent's accounts. Typically if you file a fraud alert with one agency, it notifies the others. Nevertheless, I recommend calling or contacting all three to err on the side of safety and thoroughness. An initial fraud alert is only good for 90 days. Depending on your situation, you may want to file an extended alert which is good for seven years. If identity theft is involved, you will have to provide a copy of an identity theft report that has been filed with a federal, state, or local law enforcement agency. Make sure that all documents you send to the credit reporting agencies are legible—they are picky about this. For more information about identity theft see Chapter 12.

When you talk to the credit reporting agencies, request a copy of your parent's credit report from each agency and check it for any suspicious or unauthorized activity. You can also get one free copy from each reporting agency per year from www.annualcreditreport.com. NOTE: DO NOT be taken in by clever ads urging you to get free credit reports online. Getting a report from these sites automatically enrolls you in a credit monitoring service which, if you don't cancel it within seven days, will bill you $14.95 per month. In my opinion, that's deceptive. Always go to www.annualcreditreport.com.

Please Be Extra Careful About Reloading

Reloading is when the scammers call your parent a few days or weeks after the initial scam and tell them they can help recover their lost money. They may also try to reload via email. Here's an actual reloading email a close friend of mine forwarded to me:

Hello My Dear Friend,

Your name just like mine is on the scam victims compensation list put together by the Nigeria Government Scam Victims Reconciliation Commission. I have fallen for various Scams in the past and with this compensation exercise, I have been able to bounce back to my feet. Right now I am the happiest person on earth because I have just received my own $500,000 compensation money and unlike the over $4,000 I spent dealing with wrong and fraudulent offices in the past, I spent only $205 for the paper work. This is all it will cost you to get your own money, take note of this. I will advise you to contact Rev. Father Peter Clever. He is so kind and knows just how to set things right. He works with the commission and is in charge of the on going compensation exercise. He has been trying to get in touch with you and has asked that I try to do the same when I get back to the States and I am doing just that. His email address is

_____

Cheers,

Mrs. Debra Price.

Astounding, isn't it? The scammers are attempting to capitalize on their own crimes by claiming to want to help people who have been ripped off! This also goes by the name *recovery room fraud*, as in the crooks are pretending to help a victim recover their losses. As I've written on my blog, there's no end to the clever ploys criminals use to get money out of our elderly parents and others. Notice some of the manipulative tactics here: pretending to be a scam victim to build rapport, using a woman's name in the closing to suggest trustworthiness, and even invoking the name of a priest as the clincher for being trustworthy.

Explain reloading to your parent, and tell them not to talk or respond to anyone they don't know who claims they can get their money back. Tell them to refer all calls to you. Explain that reloading is just another way the crooks try to get more money from them and keep the fraud going. This alone is a good reason to change your parent's phone numbers and maybe their email addresses. (More about changing their email addresses in a moment.)

As we've seen, the crooks are relentless and clever, so if they can get access to your parent they are likely to find a way to con them out of further money. At the end of Bill's scam ordeal, the scammers were coaching him on how to get a car title loan! They often reload by being very nice and playing off elders' loneliness, financial fears, greed, and/or desire to be helpful. Sometimes, as in Bill's case, your parent has so much invested in the con that they will keep going just to try to recover *something*. Also, once a crook has scammed your parent, they add their name to a "suckers list" of easy "marks" (victims) that they share with other crooks. Bill, for example, was being scammed by creeps from Costa Rica, Jamaica, and Canada.

Block the Criminals' Access to Your Parent

If the criminals worked your parent by phone, change your parent's phone numbers. I did this by calling Bill's wireless and landline providers. The customer service representatives I spoke with were very helpful, and didn't ask me for a copy of a power of attorney before handling the change request. Be sure to let family, friends, doctors, and the pharmacy know about the change, and post the new number near each of your parent's phones so they can learn it.

Many scams are perpetrated via email. (You've probably gotten a few suspicious emails yourself. My informal poll of ten people I know from different walks of life showed that 100 percent had received at least one email from probable scammers.) To prevent any further losses, you may have to change your parent's email address. Be sure to send a change of email address notice to friends and family, and post the new address on your parent's computer so they can learn it.

In the case of identity theft, prevent any further use of your parent's personal information through fraud alerts and credit freezes, among other things. For more details on recovery from identity theft, see Chapter 12.

Consider whether you need to involve other legal remedies to protect your parent. A restraining order, for example, could help deny a financial abuser access to your parent. Remember, the abuser has probably created a delusional belief system in your parent which allows them to keep hurting your mom or dad. If they don't have access, it's almost impossible to keep stealing.

Block Your Parent's Access to the Criminals

If your parent has been wiring money via Western Union, MoneyGram, or one of the other services of this type, you may be able to ban them from using these services. Here's what I found out about how to ban someone from Western Union:

- Write a letter explaining your relationship to the victim and the situation with the scam or fraud, along with the reason for blocking their use of the service. Be prepared to provide a copy of your power of attorney.
- The representative I spoke with told me that there is no way to completely block aliases your parent may be using to send money (yes, the scammers know this and coach their victims on how to use aliases.) Nevertheless, it's a good idea to check receipts from wire transfers to criminals for different versions of your parent's name. Include those versions of their name in the letter. For instance, if someone's name is John Allen Doe, they could send money as "Allen Doe," or even "Al Doe."
- Send the letter (return receipt requested) to:
  Western Union
  Attention: Security Department
  P.O. Box 4430
  Bridgeton, MO 63044

  Fax: 888-690-2028

In terms of the other money wiring services, be prepared for mixed, if any, results. As I was working on Step 2 of Bill's scam mess, I spent hours on hold with one company without ever speaking to someone, and was referred to the corporate office to no avail by another. If the service is in a store, you may want to ask the store manager for more details, although I once waited for over half an hour for a manager who never appeared.

The store employees I spoke with all seemed to be aware of the rampant scams affecting elders, and they said that they try to talk to the victim if they feel something is amiss. When Bill was getting ripped off, the employees of the grocery store from which he wired much of the money tried to stop him by creating a flyer with his image from the store security camera on it and posting it for the clerks to see. You may do better if you bring in a good quality photo of your parent and talk to the manager about your fears. With luck and cooperation, they may just pass along the information to their employees and prevent a scam.

Here's another thing to think about: Ask your parent if they have any convenience checks from credit card companies around the house, and look for others they may have stashed or forgotten about. These are checks that come with credit card statements or via separate mailings, usually one, two, or three at a time. Funds that these checks are written for are added to the credit card balance, and a fee is usually charged in addition to the check amount. Gather all of them you can find and shred them or put them in a safe place until they can be disposed of securely.

My recommendations to change your parent's phone numbers and email address, ban them from money wiring services, and shred their convenience checks may sound extreme. But the truth is that the criminals are so good at what they do that your parent may not be able to resist a phone call or email from them asking for more money. Better safe than sorry.

Involve the Right Authorities

Your next step, if you haven't already done it, is to file a police report. In Bill's case, the detective approached me, and the police report was a natural next step in how everything unfolded. If you've discovered the scam yourself or your parent alerted you, lock down the assets as I describe above, and then CONTACT THE POLICE IMMEDIATELY! If you're going to have any hope AT ALL of getting help, you must do this. A copy of a federal, state, or local law enforcement agency report will be required if you need to file an extended fraud alert. In addition, you have to start creating a trail of evidence to prove to creditors or the courts that your mom or dad is truly a victim of a scam or fraud. It's a part of the *due diligence* that must be done.

Further, if your situation involves your parent's wiring money overseas, the US Secret Service (http://www.secretservice.gov/) has jurisdiction. I ended up forwarding all the original receipts for the international wire transfers to the Secret Service to aid in their investigation.

Be sure to file two additional complaints: one with your state's attorney general, and one with the Federal Trade Commission (FTC). Go to this website to file a complaint with the FTC:

https://www.ftccomplaintassistant.gov/FTC_Wizard.aspx?Lang=en.

(See the appendix for contact information for your state's attorney general.)

I also recommend notifying your parent's primary care physician. As I describe in Chapter 4, the stress from going through something like this can worsen any chronic conditions your parent may have. Though it's a HIPAA violation for a healthcare worker to share medical information with you without a release from your parent, it's not a violation for you to share information with them. But it's better to ask your parent for permission to speak with their doctor, since they are likely to be very embarrassed about it.

Handling Family Member or Caregiver Financial Abuse

Based on what you find out in Step 1—especially from attorneys, Adult Protective Services workers, and experienced detectives—you may decide to confront a suspected perpetrator with your legally permissible demands. This could include having them show you documentation for all care-related expenses. If you are confronting the suspected perpetrator at your parent's home, do your best to arrange for a police officer to accompany you to prevent further theft from occurring. Someone from Adult Protective Services (APS) may be able to go with you, too. If the APS or police won't go with you, take a few other carefully chosen, levelheaded people for backup. Be careful, don't confront alone, and, naturally, observe the law at all times.

If a caregiver was exploiting your parent, speak with the Adult Protective Services folks about a "plan B" for looking after your mom or dad. An alternative care plan may involve moving your parent closer to you or arranging for other options. While none of this is easy, keeping your parent safe is the top priority. A great resource to help you with Step 2 is the National Committee for the Prevention of Elder Abuse at www.preventelderabuse.org.

Chapter 3

Step 3—Recovery: Plan Your Parent's Financial Recovery

"Planning is bringing the future into the present so that you can do something about it now."

—Alan Lakein

Now you're where the road gets steeper. In Step 3 you will be helping your parent recover financially to the extent possible. Your options for helping your mom or dad recover from the fraud will be determined in large part by how much damage was done and the way(s) the scammers ripped them off. There's no "one size fits all" plan here; rather, use my suggestions to create your own plan in collaboration with your parent and the right kinds of professionals.

By this point in the aftermath you should have a clear idea of the details of your parent's victimization. As I wrote in Chapter 1, consider the impact from multiple forms of criminal involvement, especially identity theft. Design your plan to address each one.

What are your parent's financial needs in Step 3? Does your parent face a cash crisis? Is there now a problem with credit card debt? Does your parent need to clear their name from fraudulent accounts that an identity thief set up using their personal information? Are there concerns about the integrity of their home due to a home repair scam? Although there are a few commonalities, each scam is different and requires different specific actions for recovery. You'll find more ideas specific to telemarketing, home repair, and identity theft recovery in Section Four.

Early on it is important to create a spending plan for your parent. Also known as a budget, a spending plan helps you determine whether your parent faces an immediate problem with their day-to-day expenses. There are numerous examples of spending plans online, and often a credit union or bank employee can sit down with you and develop an outline.

Continue assembling your recovery team that you began working on in Step 1 when you set up the power of attorney with your lawyer. You may or may not use the same attorney in Step 3. For Bill's recovery plan, we are using an attorney who is well versed in financial matters like credit card companies and bankruptcy instead of our elder law attorney.

Ideas to Consider When Your Parent Has a Cash Crisis

There are several options to consider if there's a problem stemming from the loss of large amounts of cash. Because I am not a professional in this area, I'm not endorsing or recommending any of them in particular; that's for you to talk over with your parent and a good financial advisor. But I do recommend that you work with a financial advisor to develop a cash-rebuilding plan. If you don't have a financial advisor, check with either The Garrett Planning Network (www.garrettplanningnetwork. com) or the National Association of Personal Financial Advisors (www.napfa.org). Your bank or credit union may also have someone on staff who can advise you about a cash-rebuilding plan.

Your parent's homeowner's insurance might cover financial losses incurred at home, and your parent might be covered for theft of items from their home, so check with the insurance agent or claims department.

Here are some ideas to explore with your financial advisor. All of them have pros and cons; some are more controversial than others. Do your homework, never enter into a financial agreement that you don't understand, and get the best advice you can. Getting more than one opinion is a good idea, too.

1. Life settlements and viatical settlements

A *life settlement* is when someone sells their life insurance policy for less than the face value of the policy, but more than the cash-surrender value, to a third-party investor(s). The third-party investor plans to profit at death of the insured person by collecting more in death benefits than they paid out for the policy (including the purchase price, transaction costs, and premiums).

Settlements of this type have been available to Americans since 1911. The financial and housing crises have caused a rise in the numbers of elderly Americans for whom their life insurance policy is now one of their more valuable assets.

A life settlement may be an option if your parent is age 70 or older and has a life insurance policy with a face value of $50,000 or more. Some independent observers estimate that over 50 percent of policies in this bracket have a market value greater than the insurance company's cash surrender value. Ask your financial advisor about this option since there has apparently been recent emphasis on training financial professionals to discuss this with clients who could possibly benefit from it.

Here are some typical criteria for the owner of a life insurance policy to become an eligible candidate for a life settlement transaction:

- Policy holders age 70 and older (ages as low as 55 are possible)
- $50,000 minimum policy face value
- Policy active for a minimum of two years

- Low policy cash surrender value
- Premiums less than 8 percent per year
- Eligible types of insurance policies:

  - Universal life

  - Term (if convertible)

  - Whole life

  - Variable life

  - Survivorship (any type)

  - Adjustable life

  - Joint first to die

Here's an example of how a life settlement could work:

- Whole life insurance

  - Male, age 75

  - Policy face amount: $1.5 million

  - Cash value: $72,000

  - Life settlement payment: $455,000

According to the Financial Industry Regulatory Authority (FINRA), life settlements can have high upfront costs, and they may cause unintended tax consequences as well as problems with programs such as Medicaid. Another big consideration is that there will be no life insurance money after your parent passes, unless they have other policies.

Viatical settlements rose to prominence in the '80s and '90s as a way for AIDS patients to access money from insurance policies for living and healthcare expenses. A viatical settlement is the same as a *life settlement*, except the insured person is terminally ill (as defined by the IRS Tax Code) with a life expectancy of less than two years.

Other options according to FINRA include borrowing against an insurance policy or taking accelerated death benefits. As always, be sure to talk these options over with your insurance, financial, and tax advisors.

2. Reverse mortgages

If your parent is at least 62 years old, you may want to take a look at a *reverse mortgage* to make up some of their losses. This is a mortgage agreement in which the homeowner receives regular payments up to the value of their home equity, and the mortgage is paid when the house is sold, usually upon the death of the homeowner. Be advised, though; reverse mortgages have some important pros and cons to consider carefully. It is especially important to think about how long your parent is likely to stay in their home. No cost and low cost reverse mortgages are available to those who anticipate moving from their home in the near future, but they carry higher interest rates than standard reverse mortgages. If your parent is unlikely to remain at the property for at least five years, a reverse mortgage probably doesn't make sense.

Reverse mortgages have been criticized for three other major shortcomings:

1. Expense: Reverse mortgages can cost $15,000 or more to enter into, as compared to other types of loans which often cost less than $10,000.

2. Confusion: Many seniors entering into reverse mortgages don't fully understand the terms and conditions associated with the loans, and critics have suggested that some lenders seek to take advantage of this.

3. <u>Compound Interest:</u> This gets complicated, but each month interest is calculated not only on the principal amount received by the borrower but on the interest previously assessed to the loan. Because of this compound interest, the longer a senior has a reverse mortgage, the more likely it is that all of their home equity will be depleted when the loan becomes due. This could be important for your parent's estate planning.

Keep in mind that with an insured Federal Housing Authority (FHA) reverse mortgage—called a home equity conversion mortgage (HECM)—the borrower can never owe more than the value of the property and cannot pass on any debt from the reverse mortgage to their heirs. The only thing the reverse mortgage lender can take is the house or property, not any other assets left in your parent's estate.

Despite the problems, in a 2006 American Association of Retired Persons (AARP) survey of people who took out a reverse mortgage, 93 percent said it had had a mostly positive effect on their lives, compared with 3 percent who said the effect was mostly negative. Ninety-three percent of borrowers also reported that they were satisfied with their experiences with lenders, and 95 percent reported that they were satisfied with the counselors they were required to see as part of the reverse mortgage process.

A reverse mortgage, while not perfect, may be a realistic option for restoring some of the cash your parent lost to the scammers. Be sure to read everything carefully and make a list of questions to ask during the required counseling sessions.

3. Options regarding your parent's home

Other options that can free up cash from home equity while avoiding the high upfront costs of a reverse mortgage include:

1. Within-family loan: You and/or other family members loan your parent the money they need to live on based on the equity in their home. A legal agreement is a must if you decide to go this way.

2. Sale-leaseback: You and/or other family members buy your parent's home and lease it back to your parent. This is another situation in which a legal agreement is absolutely essential for everyone's protection.

3. Selling and moving to a less expensive area or house: As I write this, the housing market has yet to recover, so selling your parent's home probably isn't a great idea at this time. They likely won't get a decent price even if they can sell it. Besides, most elders want to remain in their home, and moving them is usually very stressful and potentially harmful to them. Studies conducted by various agencies including AARP show that over 80 percent of elderly homeowners do not want to move. Currently there is a coordinated government program called Aging in Place intended to assist homeowners who wish to remain in their home and/or neighborhood. You may want to take a look at this website for more information: www.ageinplace.org.

4. Home equity line of credit (HELOC) requiring interest-only payments for ten years: These loans typically have very low or zero upfront costs. Watch out, though, because HELOC interest rates are usually based on the prime lending rate and are therefore often higher than those for other loans. The interest rate is also typically adjustable, so if interest rates go up, the rate for the line of credit goes up as well.

I cannot say it enough: All of these options can be fraught with problems for you and peril for your parent. *Getting great legal and financial advice is an absolute must if you decide to explore any of these options!*

As I've always heard about investing, if you don't understand it, don't do it.

4. Selling assets such as jewelry, collections, property, etc.

No one likes to think about this option, but getting ripped off definitely counts as one of those proverbial rainy days. Depending on the kinds of items or property your parent owns, they may be able to raise significant amounts of cash by selling assets.

You'll need to think in terms of calling in some different kinds of experts to help you with this, such as:

- Real estate appraisers
- Jewelry appraisers
- Reputable auctioneers
- Antique appraisers

You may want to call on other types of specialty appraisers for assets like coins and collectibles. Depending on where you live, these folks may be hard to find, and, naturally, they require payment for their services. You can conduct research about the value of your parent's assets on sites such as Ebay, but I think you do so at your own risk.

Selling assets should be a last option in truly dire circumstances. Unless your parent has wanted to get rid of them for a long time or just doesn't want them anymore, it can be very painful. And the economic downturn of the last several years has depressed prices for many types of collectibles. Do your best to work things out in another way if you can.

Credit and Debit Card Problems

If your parent was scammed using credit or debit cards, talk to the people in the investigations department at the issuing bank.

(Remember to log everything!) Call the customer service number on the back of the credit card and ask for the number for investigations. Tell them the story, and remember, your parent has been the victim of a CRIME.

Here's a rare bit of good news: If the crooks used an existing account belonging to your parent, federal law limits the losses your mom or dad will have to cover to $50. Even better, banks and credit card companies almost always waive the $50 if you prove the charges on the cards are fraudulent.

The crucial details are *who used the card* and *the type of card involved*. If the thief used your parent's credit card number, your parent is likely protected from further obligation. If your parent used the credit card to get cash advances to wire to the crooks overseas, your *parent* is a crime victim, *but the bank is not*. In my experience, banks aren't particularly helpful in these cases.

If the crime involves a debit card, your parent has fewer protections. Debit cards are covered under different laws than credit cards, and this makes debit card fraud much harder and more complicated to deal with. As attorney Mari J. Frank writes in *The Complete Idiot's Guide to Recovering from Identity Theft*:

"When you use a credit card...you receive a billing statement either in the mail or online and you have the opportunity to dispute charges. However, when you use a debit card...the fraudster will get the funds before you have time to dispute it." (p. 85).

If identity theft is involved, your parent may have more protection than you think. Chase, for example, offers zero-percent fraud liability for many, if not all, situations. Again, I can't tell you for sure because your situation is different from mine, but always ask.

Scammed

What to Do When Your Parent Used Credit Card Cash Advances to Send Money

If your parent claims they don't have any money, it's quite common for the criminals to coach them on ways to get more cash to keep the scam going. Criminals who perpetrate scams against the elderly know that most seniors have built up good credit over a lifetime and often have access to cash through one or more credit cards. Crooks are very adept at sounding helpful; they "really want [your parent] to get the big payday." This is a particularly revolting tactic.

In Bill's case, the crooks coached him on using credit card cash advances to get the money to send to them. This means we have a pile of debt to work through. Your situation will probably be different, but the principles are the same: Don't give up, use your anger and fear to negotiate a plan, and STICK TO IT unless there is a good reason to be flexible. There are more twists and turns on this road than you can imagine, so hold on!

Be a Tough Negotiator, or Call in the Cavalry

It's your job now to protect your parent from a different kind of predator: credit card companies—often large banks. If you just aren't cut out for this sort of thing, ask your attorney to handle it for you. It will cost your parent, but you may decide it's worth it.

So what can you do? You can try the straightforward approach first, explaining what happened, but don't expect much more than a few sympathetic words from the fraud investigators. I tried playing one bank against another—good cop, bad cop style: When talking to bank A, tell them bank B has been very helpful and compassionate, eager to give your parent a break. It may not be pretty, but this is about saving your loved one's future. I was able to achieve some modest results this way.

Being kind and polite when speaking with the credit card company employees isn't just the right thing to do, it can work in your favor. I talked to numerous people as I worked through this (document everything in your dealings with the credit card companies—you'll need it later), and all of them were just employees hired to deal with the mess from these crimes. Treat them with respect and courtesy, and they are more likely to put in a good word for your parent's plight. I've also found they will sometimes give great, unsolicited, off-the-record advice if you are nice to them. I got some interesting advice from an employee at one of the big banks—he was the first person who told me the banks don't view the kind of scam Bill got trapped in as a crime, at least not against them. Bill was a crime victim, but the bank was not. Therefore they wouldn't help much. It was disheartening to hear, but I was glad to know the truth.

You might get lucky and learn that they will work out a settlement for a percentage of the amount owed. This will have consequences, too, such as closing the account and a reduced credit score. I suggest you don't settle for the bank's first offer, which will typically be around 80 percent of the amount owed. And don't accept any settlement offer without having your lawyer review the proposal. From my research with the Federal Trade Commission and a local collection agency owner, I learned that a reasonable range for a settlement is anywhere from 25 to 70 percent of the amount owed, but there are no guarantees, and your situation may be different.

Once you've figured out the losses and started the process with the credit card companies, it's time to start looking at all your options. Even before you know about a possible settlement or how it might turn out, review your parent's assets. Figure out if they have anything they can sell that would make losing their good credit rating unnecessary.

Be careful about using debt settlement companies. Many of them claim to be non-profit, but they charge high fees and give little, if any value for their promises. You and your parent are better off finding a reputable credit counseling agency and having a certified credit counselor take an in-person look at your parent's situation. You can find a good credit counseling agency through your parent's financial institution, a local consumer protection agency, or the U.S. Cooperative Extension Service at http://www.csrees.usda.gov/Extension/.

Could Your Parent Need Cash More Than a Good Credit Score?

Dealing with a fraud or scam against your parent or other loved one often takes you into some hard places emotionally, and even ethically. Most of us walk through life only marginally aware of agonizing choices between a bad option and a worse one until we face one ourselves. This kind of dilemma happens frequently as you work through your recovery plan in Step 3.

One elderly man I know ended up with a pile of debt from using credit card cash advances to fund a vicious series of scams. He got caught in the illusion of the big payday waiting for him after one more payment to the criminals. When the whole thing blew up, he was left with tens of thousands of dollars in high-interest credit card debt. The credit card companies (two of the biggest banks in the country, by the way) raised the victim's interest rates from around 18 percent to *over 45 percent* on the balances. Credit card companies could do that until recent reforms went into effect.

As the man's daughter helped him sort things out, their attorney presented them with this idea: Your parent needs cash more than they need a good credit score. He suggested they consider not paying the balances. This goes against the grain for those who were rightly taught to pay their bills on time. Still, the lawyer had a point. The victim was in his late seventies. He had numerous health issues and would likely need his modest cash reserves to pay for end-of-life care.

Paying off the exorbitant amount of debt plus the inexcusably high interest would leave him dangerously low on money. The credit card companies were mostly unsympathetic and unhelpful since the crime was committed against the person and not the credit card companies. His credit score would naturally go from excellent to terrible in a few short weeks, but he needed cash reserves more than he needed a good credit score.

This strategy involves risks, and I am not suggesting anyone deliberately refuse to pay a debt or break the law. The family in this example is hoping for a reasonable settlement with the credit card issuers, but the companies wouldn't even talk to them about it until the accounts were at least 90 days past due. Talk about a weird situation!

If you find yourself and your parent in a similar predicament, consider the possibility that your parent may need cash more than a good credit score. Get good advice from an attorney and a financial advisor. Don't let you or your parent be intimidated by high-pressure tactics from credit card companies or collection agencies. Talk things over with your parent and involve them in the decision as much as possible. Keep in mind that recovering from a fraud involves several kinds of losses. One of them might be your parent's credit score.

Taxes and Scam Losses

Did you know your parent's scam-related losses and expenses are usually tax deductible? I didn't know it either until I started helping Bill handle the aftermath of his scam. The IRS lumps scam losses in with casualties, disasters, and other kinds of losses.

I spoke with Bart Stansfield, who is a certified tax preparer and an enrolled agent with the IRS. He said scam losses are considered bad debts or personal losses, and this applies even if cash advances were used to send money offshore. Use IRS Schedule D, and list the entire amount of the loss on the form. Losses offset tax liability, so if your mom or dad doesn't file a tax return this won't help, but if they do, they can offset tax liability by up to $3,000 per year until the total amount of the loss has been applied. This can help offset gains from other transactions like sales of stocks or other assets to replenish cash losses from the fraud or scam.

Here are the documentation requirements:

- The date you discovered the property was missing
- That the property was stolen
- That your parent was the owner of the property
- Whether a claim for reimbursement exists for which there is a reasonable expectation of recovery

What will cover all of these requirements? According to Bart Stansfield, *a police report and/or a complaint filed with your state's attorney general.* By now you know how important it is to document everything as you work through scam recovery. I also strongly encourage filing a police report and a complaint with your attorney general. The IRS requirements add another reason to take these steps.

Deducting scam losses won't make up for the pain of the violation and betrayal, and it won't make your parent's money reappear. Nevertheless, it may help cushion the financial hit your parent has taken. As always, please remember that I'm not a CPA or attorney, and be sure to check with your own tax preparer or accountant for the specifics in your case.

Here's the link to the IRS publication you'll need for scam losses, number 547: http://www.irs.gov/pub/irs-pdf/p547.pdf

To claim the deduction for identity-theft-related expenses, file IRS Form 4684, Casualties and Thefts. The form is divided into two parts: Part A is for personal losses. Here's the link to the instructions: http://www.irs.gov/pub/irs-pdf/i4684.pdf

Beware of one potential pitfall concerning taxes and scam losses: If you successfully negotiate a reduction in credit card debt involved in your parent's scam, the IRS considers the reduction a form of income, subject to taxation.

Because the tax code may have changed since I wrote this, always double check the information with your tax professional or the IRS. I hope this helps make this part of your recovery journey a little less overwhelming and "taxing."

Some Final Thoughts

One more important action to take: Monitor your parent's mail for at least a year after their victimization. As I mentioned earlier, the crooks will put your parent's name on a "suckers list" that they will sell to their criminal colleagues. If the crooks have your parent's mailing address, that will be on the list, too. Watch your parent's mail for phony offers and "prizes." These usually come from somewhere abroad so they can be easy to spot and toss or shred. I was amazed at how many of these showed up in Bill's mail during the first year after his scam came to light.

How long should it take to recover from a scam? Unfortunately there's no definite answer to that. Sometimes it's only a few days. More often it takes months or years.

It is possible to recover, at least somewhat, after an elderly parent gets scammed. We continue to work the plan for Bill's recovery that we developed in our own Step 3, imperfect as it is. I know the steps work based on our experience so far. You have to be flexible, and adapt to circumstances, but they work.

Are things the same for Bill as before the crimes? No, not really. He's lost a pile of money and his credit is ruined, not to mention some of his sense of safety in the world and a degree of peace of mind.

Scammed

He lives more lean, and is more careful than ever about expenses. He had some stress-related worsening of his physical health, though it seems to be improving over time. He's also extremely careful about any hint of frauds or scams coming his way because he knows he's still on the crooks' suckers list.

While getting ripped off is an ugly and painful experience, I think it's important for you and your parent to remember that there are many things the scammers never could (and never will) steal—quality of life based on enjoying time with family and friends, savoring the beauty of springtime, a hearty laugh, or a day of feeling especially good.

Money is useful, and the things and experiences it can buy often add to our lives. Still, Bill's and my experience of getting scammed reminds us that we have so much for which to be grateful, and that life is still worth living. Wherever you are in your parent's recovery, I hope you'll keep that in mind, too.

SECTION TWO

Emotional Challenges and the Psychology of Scamming

Chapter 4
Helping Your Parent Recover Emotionally

"The attitudes and beliefs of others around us have a dramatic impact on feelings of self-worth, motivations to be active and productive, and personal satisfaction with life."

—Eisdorfer and Cohen, *Integrated Textbook of Geriatric Mental Health*

As you'd expect (or may be learning), getting ripped off in a scam is a very distressing event. Our parents worked hard for many long years to create whatever level of retirement savings and comfort they have. Becoming a victim of criminals sets off an ugly array of emotions and reactions that can leave them in worse health and with an overwhelming array of painful emotions. Like just about everything concerning the aftermath of a fraud, dealing with these emotions is not easy. But there are some things you can do to help your parent recover emotionally.

Two Forms of Distress from Fraud and Scam Victimization

Betrayal of trust and having any part of your life savings and financial security stolen from you produces two kinds of stressors, *internal* and *external*. Internal stressors are what I call the "inside jobs," because they arise from within the person. They are somewhat or mostly involuntary, at least in their origins.

Internal Stressors

Examples of internal emotional stressors are sadness, guilt, shame, and fear.

The worsening of health and/or mental health from fraud victimization creates another internal stressor. In a very real way, the criminals threaten our parents' physical well-being. Here's a list of problems distress can make worse, taken from *Senior Journal*:

- Pain
- Heart disease
- Digestive problems
- Sleep problems
- Depression and anxiety
- Diabetes
- Autoimmune diseases such as arthritis

According to a study by the National Institute of Justice quoted in Les Henderson's book *Crimes of Persuasion*, 14 percent of financial fraud victims experienced physical or mental health problems directly related to their victimization. Some researchers even claim a connection between distress and certain forms of cancer.

The first step is for your parent to have a thorough medical checkup. This is important to check on whether any of their health conditions have gotten worse due to the distress of being victimized. A mental status exam to detect possible early stages of Alzheimer's disease or other cognitive deterioration may also be indicated.

Typically your parent's physician will conduct what's called a Mini-Mental® State Examination (MMSE), although you may also want to assess your parent by using the Eight-Item Informant Interview to Differentiate Aging and Dementia© (AD8). You can find the link to get a copy in Chapter 12. For more about using the AD8 as part of a thorough assessment, see Chapter 7.

Loss, Grieving, and Sadness

Getting hurt in a fraud or scam leads not only to financial losses but to the loss of qualities like trust in the world and the belief that other people are generally safe. This occurs especially when the scammer seemed like a friend, or worse, a romantic partner (as in the so-called Romeo Rip-off). A similar terrible loss occurs when the abuser is a family member.

Other losses from getting scammed include the loss of self-esteem, self-confidence, and a sense of security. Fraud victims can lose faith in their own judgment when they come to grips with the magnitude of their victimization and feel a crushing sense of shame. In addition to the fraud's impact on their future financial security, elders may have a profound fear of losing the security of their independence and control over their life. All of these are very important to your parent's sense of themselves, and are why fraud victimization is so emotionally devastating.

When we experience losses we go through grieving. The grieving process is different for everyone and for different kinds of losses. The predictable, comforting routine of life and its expectations has been taken from your dad or mom in an act of financial violation. They've been robbed! As part of the grieving process, expect them to be sad, angry, scared, hurt, and all the combinations of these you can think of. They are going through a *normal reaction* to an *extraordinary* event.

Here's a little good news: While most people go through a reactive depression after a distressing event, they also eventually find ways to deal with their loss and grieving with help from those around them and by using healthy coping strategies. Your help and support is important to your parent's emotional recovery.

Guilt and Shame

Guilt is feeling badly because you did something wrong. It is usually accompanied by a sense of responsibility and remorse for what happened. Shame, on the other hand, is a feeling of disgrace which, in the world of counseling and psychotherapy, more often refers to a state of being. A person feels *guilty* because they did something, while *shame* reflects a state of being defective and/or worthless.

One of the toughest internal stressors a victimized parent faces is excessive self-blame driven by anger-fueled guilt and shame. This is often a misguided attempt to help the situation by beating up on themselves with their self-talk. It can take the forms of unhealthy self-criticism ("What is wrong with me?") and harsh self-judgment ("I must be an idiot"), among others.

We all know we get ourselves into messes sometimes, and sometimes those messes are pretty big deals. Of course we feel terrible about what we did, and wish we could do it over. Acknowledging and "owning" our part in creating a predicament for ourselves is healthy; we can then work productively on correcting the mess. It's NEVER productive or healthy to keep the blaming going. We have to choose our thoughts to drown out the negative voices in our heads.

Regret and remorse can haunt your parent for a long time. Sometimes it helps to remind them that the criminals who hurt them are professionals and that they are incredibly good at what they do. Some psychologists say they are better at what they do than we are at protecting ourselves. They are intelligent, and as well educated in their dirty work as any lawyer, doctor, or accountant.

Fear

Fear ranges from mild anxiousness about the outcome of the scam recovery plan to phobic reactions about leaving the house and even symptoms similar to those of post-traumatic stress disorder (PTSD). Perhaps the most common fear reaction is worry: "What if I can't live on what's left of my money?"

Several factors help reduce anxiety in this situation. First and probably foremost is the emotional and social support you extend to your parent. It's vitally important that your parent not feel alone with such an overwhelming life event. You, along with other trusted family and friends, are in the best position to help your parent reduce their fear. We are social creatures, and the relationships your parent has can be enormously helpful in how well they get through the aftermath of a scam or fraud. Asking for and receiving help from concerned and competent professionals is part of your support strategy.

Another helpful anxiety- and fear-reducing factor is having good information. Not knowing what's going on allows the fearful parts of our brains to run wild. You can combat fear and anxiety by using the processes in this book to gather details about the nature and extent of the crime(s) against your parent.

The third way to cope with fear is to create a plan. Uncertainty about what to do to resolve a problem leads to far too many "what-ifs," a hallmark of anxious thinking. Use the ideas and suggestions in this book to formulate your scam recovery plan. Keep looking for the support, information, and plan that best helps your parent recover.

Ways to Help

What are some of the ways you can help reduce the impact of distress on your mom or dad? Here are some ideas for minimizing internal stressors:

Let your parent tell their story. They may feel the need to do this over and over. This is a normal part of coming to terms with what's happened.

- Tell your parent you're sorry this happened to them and you're going to help them get through it.

- Don't blame, lecture, or call your parent names like "foolish," or "stupid."

- Help your parent remember this: "DON'T BLAME YOURSELF FOR MORE THAN TEN MINUTES. PUT THE BLAME WHERE IT BELONGS—WITH THE CROOKS WHO RIPPED YOU OFF." As their family member, you'll do better if you remember this, too.

- Never talk about your lost inheritance.

- Remind your parent and yourself that there's no such thing as a "little" fraud or scam. Some people lose thousands of dollars, others a few hundred or less. Everyone who gets ripped off hurts.

- Encourage your parent to choose their thoughts. Have them repeat, both out loud and to themselves, words like this: "I made a mistake. I choose to move on with my life." You'll be surprised at how effective this can be for many people.

- Don't threaten to take over their finances.

- Let your parent talk about their feelings, completely and honestly. Invite them to open up as much as they want to, and keep encouraging them to be honest. If your parent feels they did something stupid, give them the safety to admit it. Remember, you've probably done some things you regret in your life, too.

- **<u>DO NOT JUDGE YOUR PARENT FOR WHAT HAPPENED!</u>** As I tell my clients: When we're judging, we're not helping. Being judgmental about things blocks the feeling of safety in the relationship, separates you from your parent emotionally, and adds to their distress. I think it also lessens the likelihood of a positive outcome.

- Help your parent calm themselves with music, movies, crafts, hobbies, and other healthy distractions.

- Let your parent vent all the "if onlys." They're normal, and a part of how they'll heal from this.

- Don't let your parent make themselves crazy trying to figure out why their "friend" did this to them. The only answer is that's what crooks do—they rip off good and decent people. For more about the psychology of frauds and scams, see Chapter 6.

- The same is true for the "Why did this happen to me?" dead end. Consider what personal vulnerabilities contributed to the problem only in the interest of learning from them and practicing better prevention. Don't let it become a repetitive loop.

- Redirect your parent toward problem solving and coping in the here and now. Do this with your words and actions. Model for your parent that they may be a victim, but they are taking steps to deal with problems (with your help). There's a big difference between the fact of victimhood and getting stuck in the victim mindset.

- Encourage your parent to truly get on with their life. This is why Step 3 is about making and executing a recovery plan. Live in today, set a goal, and go after it with single-minded determination.

- Getting on with life also means enjoying life again to the fullest extent possible. Take your parent out to favorite places, bring the grandchildren around more often, and maybe even get them laughing again. While the fraud is bad, don't let it take over all of life. Take breaks from it!

External Stressors

External stressors are the forces and realities imposed on us from our surroundings or environment. Examples of these include dealing with police or other law enforcement personnel, banks and other financial institutions, and the reactions of others. Often these are harder to deal with than internal stressors because we have limited control over them.

Keep in mind that the process of scam recovery *takes time*. As I write this in early 2012, we are still working on the recovery plan for Bill's scam—almost three years after it came to light. Don't stress yourself and your parent with unrealistic time pressures. Feeling in a hurry after the initial crisis can lead to ineffective plans and outcomes.

Here are some ideas for handling external stressors:

- Recommend that your parent choose carefully whom they talk to about the fraud. If they have family members or friends who are good listeners, they should be your parent's first choice. Less is more when it comes to folks who are judgmental, condescending, or coldly unsympathetic. Willingly accept your ability to influence who has contact with your mom or dad, especially early in the recovery process. Don't let them be judged by anyone.

- Choosing carefully whom your parent talks to goes for law enforcement officers and officials from financial institutions, too. Bill and I were fortunate to work with a great detective as the full extent of the scam came to light. My experience with employees of banks and credit card companies was considerably more mixed. Some were awesome, doing everything they could and even offering me priceless off-the-record advice. Others were seriously unhelpful or just plain incompetent. I think it's best for you to talk to these people instead of your parent if at all possible so that such people don't make things worse for your mom or dad. Ask to speak to a different person if you're getting nowhere with the one you're working with.

- If your parent is fearful or anxious about experiencing a cash crunch, review Step 3 in Chapter 3. Remind them of what you've come up with in collaboration with your attorney, financial planner, and/or other professionals. Reexamine the plan and tweak it if something big has changed, like their house or car suddenly needs some major repair.

Watch for Signs of Depression and Anxiety Disorders

Depression is the most common mental health problem in elders. Researchers believe there is a spectrum of depressive illnesses in elders that ranges from the barely noticeable to major, full-blown forms of clinical depression and bipolar disorder. A type of depression that does not fit a set of criteria for a separate diagnostic category is called "depressive disorder NOS (not otherwise specified)," which can be caused by a number of factors. A significant number of elder scam victims probably fit this description. Here are a few of the indicators for depressive disorder NOS:

- Sadness
- Loss of interest in formerly pleasurable activities
- Problems sleeping
- Loss of appetite/weight loss
- Loss of energy and motivation
- Agitation or slowed-down motion
- Problems with memory and concentration
- Guilt
- Thoughts of death

Depressive disorder may present with different symptoms in seniors than in younger people. Here are some differences to watch for:

- Lack of sadness
- Anxiety/panic symptoms
- Bodily symptoms such as increased aches, pains, headaches, stomach/gastrointestinal difficulties, etc., known as "masked depression with somatization."

(The preceding information is from: Eisdorfer, Carl; Cohen, Donna (2011-07-20). *Integrated Textbook of Geriatric Mental Health* (Kindle location 3266). Johns Hopkins University Press. Kindle edition)

Another kind of mental disturbance to watch for in your parent after scam victimization is anxiety disorders. As discussed in the section called "Fear" above, these range from mild anxiousness about the outcome of the scam recovery plan to phobic reactions about leaving the house and even symptoms similar to those of post-traumatic stress disorder. If your parent had a tendency to be nervous or a worrier before, expect it to get at least temporarily worse after a scam.

Since a range of reactions to the distress of being victimized is normal, how do you know if you should be concerned? Two ways are by noticing how long the reactions last, and whether they worsen over time. Experts say symptoms that last more than four to six weeks signal a need for evaluation for treatment, especially if they become increasingly debilitating.

Supporting Resilience in Your Parent after a Fraud

One of the most exciting topics of psychological study is that of *resilience*, which refers to the ability to bounce back after adversity. Researcher Ann S. Masten describes what she calls a "steeling effect" in which a person who suffers a setback actually ends up functioning better than before it happened.

There is so much exciting information about resilience that a comprehensive overview of ways to support resilience in your parent after a fraud is beyond the scope of *Scammed* But here are some basic ideas for building resilience as you help your parent:

- Safety: Make sure your parent knows about the ways you are working to keep them safe from further victimization and negative consequences. Ensure that your relationship with them stays emotionally safe and as free from hurtful criticism and judgment as possible.
- Connection: Show your parent that they are dearly loved by you and other family members. Encourage emotionally safe people to spend time with them.

- Efficaciousness: This is a combination of your parent *feeling competent*, and feeling *confident* in their competence. You can support efficaciousness by letting them help with the recovery process as much as possible, and showing appreciation for their ideas and help.
- The ability to calm oneself: This means your parent's sense of being able to reduce anxiety and other distress through practices such as those discussed earlier in this chapter.
- Optimism: Tell your parent you have a realistically hopeful belief that they will recover as much as possible after the scam. Give them specific reasons you believe this to be true.

A final thought about the emotional side of recovery comes from the world of positive psychology. In his book *The Happiness Advantage: The Seven Principles of Positive Psychology That Fuel Success and Performance at Work,* author and researcher Shawn Achor writes:

"Simply speaking, the human psyche is so much more resilient than we even realize…we consistently forget how good our psychological immune system is at helping us get over adversity."

The emotional effects of getting ripped off can be hard to handle. You, as your parent's helper and advocate, hold the keys to creating the best possible outcome for them. I hope this chapter has helped you begin to see that you, and the right people around you, can make a huge difference in how your parent gets through the fallout from getting ripped off.

Chapter 5

Handling Your Own Emotions: The Importance of Good Self-Care

"You have to take care of yourself. If you don't take care of yourself, you won't be able to take care of another person."
—Claire Berman, *Caring for Yourself While Caring for Your Aging Parents: How to Help, How to Survive* [3rd ed.]

Your role as your parent's lifeline to reality and recovery depends on your ability to handle your own emotions and keep your goal of protecting your parent topmost in your mind. Of course you're angry, scared, and frustrated! Your challenge is to use those emotions to work towards the most constructive possible resolution of the situation. Do this by creating safety, awareness, and collaboration with your parent. This is a form of rapport-building, which is how you influence your parent to see what's really going on and to help you help them.

Finding out that your parent or other loved one has been ripped off by a scammer is a huge deal. You're just so *angry* about it! How could this have happened?! Then, as they say on those cheesy TV ads, "But wait! There's more!" How about the *fear?* You wonder if your dad or mom will still be OK financially, emotionally, and even in terms of their physical well-being. Mixed in with all that are feelings of being *overwhelmed*, and sometimes *helplessness, confusion,* and *guilt.* You may also be *sad* to see the fallout from being victimized in your parent and others in your family. There's no doubt about it; you have a lot on your plate when you're helping your parent recover. What will help you? Self-care.

Self-care refers to a series of choices you make to ensure you continue to function or perform at your best. It includes behaviors and chosen thoughts or attitudes designed to minimize stress and maximize your energy for flexible and adaptive problem solving. Good self-care is essential for everyone, especially in times of extraordinary stress.

The Basics of Self-care

At all times, but especially when you're helping your parent recover after a fraud or scam, be sure you get enough rest and physical activity. Both are sources of energy for most people, and are vital for your performance. Physical activity is a free anti-depressant, without the side effects.

Remember to eat lean proteins, whole grains, and fresh fruits and vegetables, since nutrition experts say that these foods most efficiently feed your brain and body. Avoid eating a lot of sugar and white carbs; they make your energy and focus crash shortly after eating them. Watch your alcohol and caffeine intake, too. Refuse the cheap fix they seem to offer, which mostly just makes you feel worse after a little while. In a way, you are running a mental/emotional marathon when you are helping your parent after a scam, and I encourage you to feed yourself like an athlete.

Handling Your Anger

It's very normal for us to become upset during the discovery and aftermath of a fraud against our parent. Anger is a natural and healthy response to insults and violations. It's a way we mobilize ourselves to take effective action to defend or protect. Handling anger skillfully can be very difficult, though, because we all have the human tendency to become judgmental. This is especially true in situations that could have been prevented, such as when a parent gets taken by a scam artist.

When I talk about handling anger skillfully, what I mean is channeling and using the anger to move forward and solve a problem. This is a big part of why I'm writing this book; I want you to have helpful information and ideas to move forward with the recovery process and solve the problem of your parent's victimization. A part of this is to use your natural tendency to get angry in ways that help, not hurt, your parent, the situation, and yourself.

When anger turns to judgment or being judgmental, it separates us from the other person involved and condemns them as "stupid," "crazy," or whatever negative word flies out of our mouths. *This is exactly the opposite of what's helpful.* Your mom or dad is already feeling scared, angry, and maybe ashamed or stupid after the fraud comes to light. Reinforcing these emotions by judging them adds to their stress and blocks their ability to be of much help to you. If they can't or won't help you by answering questions or finding paperwork, your job will be that much harder.

What *is* likely to be better and more helpful is to stop yourself from judging your parent. Of course you're upset and angry and scared. These feelings are normal in the aftermath of a scam. Use your anger to fuel your determination to handle things well. Talk to or vent to a different family member or friend. Speak with your therapist, counselor, or religious leader. If no one's available, write down all your angry thoughts on a piece of paper and throw it away. Research shows that for most people, talking about upsetting things with another caring person actually reduces levels of stress hormones in the brain. Daniel Siegel, M.D., in his marvelous book, *Mindsight,* calls this phenomenon "Name it to tame it."

Let me normalize something else for you right now: You can be as pissed off as you want to at the crooks who did this to your parent; they are predators, and beneath contempt. Having said this, *don't let it consume you.* As you know, being angry at them isn't going to help your parent get their money or property back. Channel your anger into effective action. Want more than that? Take a look at the scambuster/scambaiter community online at websites like www.scambaiters.com.

I have a confession to make: I have been a scambaiter. A few months after Bill's scam came to light, I got a text message purportedly from a local credit union. It said my account had some sort of problem with it, and I needed to call an 800 number to correct it. The funny thing was I didn't even have an account with that credit union!

This happened on a weekend, when I have unlimited cell phone minutes, so I thought I'd have a little fun. I blocked my number, even though I knew they must already have it. I called the 800 number, and a recorded voice informed me that my call "may be recorded for quality purposes." Yeah, right. When the voice told me to enter my account number, I proceeded to tie up the scammers' phone line for over half an hour entering sequences of repeated numbers like 3333-3333-3333-3333. I'll never know for sure, but I hope my foray into scambaiting prevented someone else from getting ripped off. To top it off, I felt a delicious sense of power at being able to strike back in some small way.

Adjust Your Thinking to Soothe Your Emotions

To reduce your upset, think about the situation in a different but still realistic way. My friend and colleague Dr. Jennifer Abel, in her book *Active Relaxation,* calls this "finding the B3s"—Better But Believable ideas.

For example, consider that your parent's stubborn denial may actually be rooted in fear—especially the fear of loss. Losing control is a huge factor that haunts elders. Your parent may be fearful of losing the connection they think they have with the scammer and returning to dreary loneliness. Your dad or mom may be afraid of losing the dream about a big payday, being able to relax about money, and maybe even leaving a little something for their loved ones after their death. Your parent may be frightened of the possibility that they are wrong about the criminals being nice people, and what that could mean for their own future ("Am I losing it?").

By finding "Better But Believable" ideas, you can look at the situation with more compassion. Greater compassion and concern makes it easier to focus your interactions with your parent in the direction of connecting with them to help them. Helping your parent and yourself get over the scam is what it's all about, especially in the early stages of recovery. Keep that front and center in your mind and action at all times.

Self-care in a Time of Unwanted Change

Another way to think about self-care while you're helping your parent cope with scam victimization is within the framework of handling unwelcome change. If ever there were a situation that qualifies as unwelcome or unwanted change, it would be dealing with your parent's victimization!

I recently read an article based on a book by M.J. Ryan called *AdaptAbility: How to Survive Change You Didn't Ask For,* since many (most?) of my clients face those kinds of changes. It occurred to me that her material contains ideas for helping us help our parents in scam situations as well. Here are a few:

- Participate in one activity every day that you can control completely.
- Act as if you have the skills and confidence needed to handle the situation, and soon you will.

- Think about where you want your parent and you to be a year from now. Recent research from the field of positive psychology shows that people who mentally practice the best outcomes actually feel hopeful and more positive.
- Pay big attention to small successes.
- Consider why different options might work, even if you fear they won't.
- Encourage yourself, out loud if possible.
- Schedule a fifteen-minute worry time every day to isolate this emotion from the rest of your day.
- Remind yourself about your strengths and good qualities every time you feel stress about the scam. (I would add to that thinking of your parent's good qualities and what you love about them, too.)

Contain the Damage

Collateral damage is a term the military uses to describe damage that occurs unintentionally to civilians from weapons aimed at other targets. A story I heard not long ago about a friend's pastor's downfall started me thinking about the collateral damage from frauds and scams against elders. My friend had been very close to the pastor and his wife because they had helped her through some tough times. She was shocked and saddened to find out that he was accused of scamming several older members of his congregation out of significant sums of money.

Such damage includes feeling personally violated or betrayed, losing trust in people in a broad sense, uncomfortable feelings that the world isn't really as safe as we thought, and/or harsh and unrealistic self-judgments ("I'm so stupid for letting this happen to Mom!").

Similar feelings arise even more powerfully when a family member, close friend, or caregiver is the perpetrator of the fraud. We can't imagine that the person who hurt our parent is also the one who was supposed to be looking out for them. It's shocking, and can leave us numb at first, then full of rage and a desire for revenge later. If we're not careful, we can end up bitter and resentful, and full of hostility that can damage more than just our emotional well-being.

So what can we do about collateral damage? In addition to the ideas I presented earlier in this chapter, remember to keep your thinking *specific*. Strong emotional states color our perceptions of ourselves, the world, and others. Train your thoughts by using choice-driven repetition to come back to the *specific person and what they did* and away from "the world is a terrible place, all people suck, and I'm a loser because I didn't know about it or stop it in time."

Always come back to problem solving and planning to reduce the negative effects on you and your parent. This might include a more robust plan for preventing future victimization, and might help *you* to help *others*. Most of us feel better when we help other people.

Forgiving Your Parent

It's amazing to me how controversial the idea of forgiveness can be for people. Some folks believe forgiveness cheapens the need for accountability and even blame when someone messes up. It's as if forgiving someone lets them off too easy. Still others seem to think they have to forgive even the most heinous violations without regard to appropriate acknowledgment of the harm caused.

I come down strongly on the side of situationally appropriate forgiveness. I don't think there's a "one size fits all" approach to forgiveness for every type of wrongdoing; however, when it comes to your scam-victimized parent, I think forgiveness is definitely the way to go.

As your parent works through the denial and fully realizes what's happened to them, they are likely to feel terrible about putting you, other family members, their care team, and their recovery team through all the recovery tasks. Even if they've been an unwitting victim of identity theft, they are still likely to feel very guilty because they "should have known," or "shouldn't have let this happen." This is the time to remind your dad or mom once again that they are a *victim of a crime, not an accomplice.* Some elders (and others) get stuck in the "woulda, coulda, shoulda" part. Even if they gave money or information to a family member who seemed honest, or if they felt they didn't pay close enough attention to the signs or their intuition, they still deserve your forgiveness so they can be more at peace.

Eye Movement Desensitization and Reprocessing

Eye movement desensitization and reprocessing (EMDR) was first developed by Dr. Francine Shapiro in the late '80s and early '90s to help war veterans recover from post-traumatic stress disorder. Since then it has helped thousands of people with all kinds of problems. I've personally seen it work for what we call "big T traumas," things like combat trauma, car accidents, and rapes, but it works well for the "small t traumas," too. These are the bad things which happen to us and we "just can't quite get over them."

If you (or your parent) are having a tough time moving on from thinking about the crime – that is, you're thinking about it a lot of the time when you should be or want to be thinking about something else – consider finding a therapist trained in EMDR. Chances are it will help you (and your parent) find much more peace about what happened.

In conclusion, self-care in the aftermath of a scam or fraud is essential for the most successful and productive resolution of the mess. Handle the crisis as described in Steps 1 and 2, and then remember your parent is depending on you to help them through the fear and confusion. Taking care of you helps you take care of them.

Chapter 6

The Psychology of Scamming: An Introduction to How the Scammers Do It and What That Can Teach Us

"There can be no question that they are an unusually sick group in terms of mental health and unusually antisocial group in terms of lack of regard for others and the lack of control over their own impulses."

—Richard Blum, *Deceivers and Deceived*

The criminals who went after your mom or dad are professionals. It's their *job*, and some people claim they study their reprehensible craft day and night. Their sole purpose is to rip people off, and no doubt about it, they are very, very good at it. They seem to be as intelligent and well educated in their line of work as any doctor or lawyer is in his or her respective profession. The rest of us often underestimate them, and the crooks like it that way because it makes their jobs easier.

So why even take the time to consider the psychology of scamming? What researchers are confirming is that we do better when things make sense. When things make sense we tend to relax, which allows our innate abilities of problem solving and adaptation to kick in.

In this chapter I intend to help you understand your parent's fraud victimization so you can make more sense of the situation and not feel so powerless. It provides a foundation for the prevention ideas I discuss in Section Three. We'll consider first the psychology of the scammers themselves, followed by that of the victims. I conclude with a look at similarities between hypnotic methods and the ways the crooks carry out their crimes.

Psychological Issues of the Scammers

I haven't found much in the way of reliable research specifically on scammers' psychology. I think it's safe to say, though, that most of the people who perpetrate scams and frauds are likely *sociopaths* (also known as *psychopaths*). The term from psychology is *antisocial personality disorder*. These are the scary people who are born without a conscience. Charming, self-centered, and highly manipulative, they think nothing of hurting people because they objectify and dehumanize their victims.

According to Dr. Aaron T. Beck's book *Prisoners of Hate: The Cognitive Basis of Anger, Hostility, and Violence*, criminals view themselves as "invulnerable, superior, [and with] pre-emptive rights," which means it's all about what they want. In addition, they look at others as "dupes, inferior, [and] weak" (p.138). Our parents are literally nothing to them but a payday or even a game. Often they get an adrenaline rush from defrauding others, and a sense of triumph or victory. Put bluntly, they're predators.

Some people who perpetrate fraud are not sociopaths, but indulge in what therapists call "selective disengagement of moral self-sanction from inhumane conduct." What a mouthful! This means they use mental games to ignore internal messages meant to stop them from hurting others. I theorize that they often use worthy ends such as the need to support a family in a hostile economic environment to socially and morally justify hurting our parents. They downplay the harm they cause and even blame the victims for bringing the problems on themselves. Either way, or through a combination of these two elements, our elder loved ones don't stand a chance against these people unless we help them.

Psychological Dynamics of Victims

As part of maintaining my license to practice therapy, I have to attend a certain number of hours of continuing education every two years. I especially love it when my training encompasses both of my passions: providing excellent psychotherapy and my work with elderly scam recovery and prevention. I recently attended a couple of workshops given by Dr. Jim Fogarty about emotional manipulation that did just that.

Dr. Fogarty has some very helpful ideas about victims' erroneous thinking—what we call *cognitive distortion* in the world of psychotherapy. There are twelve to fifteen of these thinking errors, depending on whose work you're considering. Usually several cognitive distortions operate simultaneously in any given scam situation. Here's a list of several prominent ones for elderly fraud victims:

- All-or-nothing thinking, aka *splitting*: the victim thinks that a certain action or behavior is the only one possible
- Emotional reasoning: the victim believes something is true because they "feel" it is true
- Mental filtering: the victim is unable to see the negative possibility in the scam
- Catastrophizing—especially common in home repair rip-offs and the "grandchild stuck in a foreign country" scam: the victim believes the situation is extremely serious and requires immediate action

These cognitive distortions stoke what's called *magical thinking*, especially the variation called *magical solutions*. This is when someone believes the "nice person" on the phone is offering them an easy, relatively pain-free solution to a problem they have. An example of this is when a victim believes they are going to receive a larger sum of money in exchange for wiring a smaller, but still significant sum of money to someone out of the country.

Dr. Fogarty explains that cognitive distortions powerfully fuel magical thinking, making it more convincing and rigid. With the criminals' skillful manipulation, the victim thinks, "This is the *only way* I can achieve the desired solution to my problem." As the manipulation continues, the victim becomes more and more caught up in the scammers' dysfunctional, self-serving belief system. Usually the victim does what the crooks want them to do and ends up getting hurt.

To summarize: A scammer makes contact with a potential victim, then begins building a destructive delusional belief system designed to serve the criminal's desires, most often for money or information. The crook does this by deliberately sowing and reinforcing cognitive distortions and a belief in magical solutions in the victim. The victim does what the scammer wants and loses.

I also want to zoom in on another particularly evocative idea that Dr. Fogarty's work inspired for me: When an elderly person gets ripped off, it isn't about being stupid; it's often about unmet needs. Many people judge victims of frauds and scams as stupid, gullible, or some variation of these ideas. Doesn't it change a person's thinking to consider the possibility that the scam victim is really lonely, or fearful about their financial well-being, or just wants to help some poor unfortunate? I certainly hope so. In my opinion, scam victims need HELP, not judgment. I believe this idea powerfully informs good prevention, too; more about that in the next chapter.

A certain level of unmet needs in an elder is normal, so please do your best to move beyond any guilt you may feel about this. We can't possibly meet all of our needs as younger adults, let alone as we age. Virtually everyone experiences a discrepancy between their needs and what their life actually brings them. What we're seeking to do here is understand more about the role unmet needs play in our parents' vulnerability to criminals who want to use their discrepancies against them, and perhaps work with our elder loved ones to help them think more clearly and have fewer unmet needs.

The Five FLAGS: A Simple Introduction to Unmet Needs

I receive regular Google alerts about fraud against elders and related issues as part of my mission to serve in this way. A short time ago I read a story about police in Tennessee who caught some criminals who were victimizing elders. The reporter casually described a book the investigators found in the crooks' belongings entitled *The Black Science: Ancient and Modern Techniques of Ninja Mind Manipulation* by Dr. Haha Lung and Christopher Prowant. Since it isn't common to know what's on a fraudster's professional reading list, I bought the book to check it out.

To be honest, I didn't expect much from the book—the title sounds a bit sensational, and the authors' names sound contrived. Besides, it wouldn't be the first time a resource didn't prove helpful. Some of what I found, however, has become a simple, memorable introduction to several unmet needs in victims that criminals use to exploit them. I've used this material in my talks to elders and professionals with very positive feedback.

The "five FLAGS" inspired by the book are:

- Fear
- Loneliness
- Anger
- Greed
- Sympathy

Fear

We all live with fear every day. Some authors have even written about fear as a gift, and there's no doubt it serves many useful purposes. For our elder loved ones, however, the normal fears of everyday life can be magnified by losses in physical and thinking capacity, along with confusing changes in the world they've known all their lives.

For example, who would have ever thought that house prices would actually decline in the last few years, with little indication of recovery as I write this? When you add in the steadily rising costs of prescription drugs and healthcare, many elders feel very uncertain about their futures. Con artists are adept at playing off these fears, as well as others such as fear for the well-being of their children or grandchildren—as victims of the "grandchild stuck in a foreign country" scam know all too well. Of course, the elder's unmet need here is for *security*.

Scammers love to build fear and anxiety with phony urgency. A recent spate of frauds has involved the "grandchild in jail" story. The crooks gather the elderly person's personal information on the internet and then make up a story about a grandchild's being in jail in another country (often Canada or Mexico). The frantic grandparent usually doesn't think twice about wiring money to help, which of course ends up in the hands of the criminals. The grandchild was nowhere near whatever country the crooks mentioned.

Other ways scammers use fear against our parents is through tactics relating to time pressure and intimidation. Time pressure is used in the old advertising trick called "the limited-time offer." The crooks manipulate your parent to act fast, suspend judgment, and not check things out by claiming that "the prize money is only available for a short time." Research has shown that the speed at which we process information noticeably slows after age 60, which means that sound judgment, reasoning, and decision-making require a longer time. And sometimes scammers use plain, old-fashioned intimidation to get an elder to do what they want. This is especially present in face-to-face scams, such as home repair rip-offs and parking lot encounters such as the "pigeon drop," in which an elder loses a significant sum of money when it is switched for a worthless pile of paper. Intimidation over the phone is also common.

Loneliness

Isolation and loneliness is a sad fact of life for far too many seniors. The Commonwealth Fund Commission on the Elderly Living Alone indicated, based on a national telephone survey, that:

"One third of older Americans live alone and one quarter of these persons, typically older women, live in poverty and report poor health. The elderly person living alone is often a widowed woman in her eighties who struggles alone to make ends meet on a meager income. Being older, she is more likely to be in fair or poor health. She is frequently either childless or does not have a son or daughter nearby to provide assistance when needed."

AARP reports new research by Peter A. Lichtenberg of Wayne State University's Institute of Gerontology which indicates that loneliness boosts a senior's risk of falling for scams by 30 percent. Living alone doesn't always mean being lonely or isolated, but I suggest that it increases the likelihood of scam victimization as a result of not having people around to help with judging the validity of exaggerated claims that hook so many elders. The unmet need here is for *connection*.

Anger

Anger is one of the "hottest" emotions we experience. All emotions carry with them an *action imperative*, or the behavior(s) our bodies want to carry out when they experience the emotion. Often the action imperative that anger carries is tough to rein in once it gets going, because it so often has to do with defending something important (like ourselves or our loved ones). Anger's action imperative can be an impulse for revenge—to feel justice in seeing an offender hurt in a way that is similar to the way we were hurt.

For example, when fraudsters use reloading to extract more money from a victim after the first scam, they often use the anger the victim feels to get them to send more money to recover their original losses. This is frequently done in combination with triggering fear. More about how the criminals use the five FLAGS in combination below.

Greed

Who wouldn't like some free, extra money? Who doesn't like a bargain? Greed, defined as "excessive or rapacious desire, especially for wealth or possessions" (dictionary.com) ranges from mild to severe, and affects everyone at one time or another. Criminals and certain organizations and governments (think sweepstakes, lotteries, and other kinds of gambling) know how to motivate people to do things based on this all-too-human impulse and the desire to get something for nothing. Greed is a major contributor to scam losses from phony sweepstakes and contests. The crooks may also be playing off the senior's need for financial security.

Sympathy

Sympathy is one of our nobler emotions, based as it is on attachment to others. With all the suffering in the world, many people and situations merit our sincere sympathy. It's what gets us to donate to worthwhile charities or help a struggling child or grandchild.

Nevertheless, the impulse to sympathize can set us up to give to organizations and people who are sketchy at best. I have blogged about scam charities several times, always encouraging potential donors and/or their family member to check out a charity before they give money.

The exploitation of an elder's sympathy happens far too often at the hands of family, caregivers, and even professionals. Family members dealing with crushing medical debt, job loss, and the like deserve appropriate, reasonable help which takes into account the elder's financial situation. And those who are addicted or clinically depressed need effective treatment.

Great risk may be present for an elder's financial well-being from those who play on their sympathy. The MetLife Mature Market Institute, in its 2011 report entitled *The MetLife Study of Elder Financial Abuse: Crimes of Occasion, Desperation, and Predation Against America's Elders,* describes the "'Well, okay' syndrome," in which repeated financial abuse occurs as the elder keeps giving money to a family member saying, "Well, okay, just one more time…". This can lead to the elder's going without necessities in order to keep the misguided help going, and doesn't truly help the abuser.

In addition to the five FLAGS presented above, sometimes scammers use good qualities, like respect for authority and the willingness to cooperate, against our parents. While I was writing this book a friend of mine sent me a story about how crooks used these qualities to get money from people by pretending they were calling from Visa or MasterCard. The criminals told a fairly long, plausible story about a "pattern of suspicious activity" on the victim's account, then asked for the security code number on the back of their card. This was to "verify the accountholder was in possession of the card." What really happened was the scammer used the card and stuck the person for almost $500.

In my experience and observation, most of the time perpetrators use two or more of the FLAGS, perhaps along with some desirable qualities they've twisted to suit their purposes, to pull off their dirty work. Virtues such as respect for authority are powerful motivators for those in the elderly age bracket. Fraudsters will use anything and everything they can to get what they want. An overarching technique they use involves confusion. They get the victim hooked, then confused, then rip them off. Interestingly, this strategy bears some similarities to methods from therapeutic hypnosis (without the rip-off!). More about this in the next section.

Neuroscience teaches us that our emotional brain is older and larger than our thinking brain. That's why hijacking a senior's emotional brain with the five FLAGS, other hooks, and confusion is so effective. Strong emotions rooted in survival such as anger and fear particularly cloud the victim's mind. These emotions effectively get the thinking brain and its healthy skepticism and vigilance to go offline where it can't help protect the victim.

What happens in scam victimization is a collision of the elder's issues and weaknesses with the crooks' superior abilities to deceive and manipulate. As with many collisions, someone's going to get hurt. As we've seen, it's usually the elderly person.

Hypnosis and Deceptulation

As I was writing this chapter, I was also preparing a talk for a Missouri National Association of Social Workers symposium. I spoke on preventing scams against our elders, a topic as important to me as scam recovery. I've seen firsthand, and heard from many people with whom I've consulted, the devastation scammers wreak. I wanted to explain to the attendees more about the nuts and bolts of how the crooks rip off so many vulnerable people. If I can understand and explain this to my colleagues, maybe we can make a difference in terms of stopping even one older person from being hurt in this painful way.

Scammed

Daniel Goleman's book *Emotional Intelligence* came out a number of years ago, and it was groundbreaking in how it popularized the idea of a separate form of intelligence having to do with handling emotions and relationships skillfully. I wanted to incorporate the idea of teaching elders simple, memorable ways to handle certain emotions well into my talks about prevention, since it's clear to me that the scammers use emotion to manipulate their victims.

I have a long background in hypnosis as part of my work in psychotherapy and mental health. I was initially trained in hypnosis in 1983, and have continued my education in this field. It occurred to me in preparing my talks that a part of how elders get ripped off resembles hypnosis. Scammers create a destructive delusional belief system in our parents which leads them to give the scammers money and personal information. They do this by building rapport and using hypnotic methods to manipulate our parents. If we can better understand how they do this, we can prevent it more effectively.

My stepfather, Bill, and virtually every scam victim or family member I've talked to, has told me that the scammers always sound like the nicest, most helpful people you'd ever want to meet. This phony warmth and interest in an elder is how the crooks build rapport, meeting the victim's unmet needs for companionship and concern from another. If you know many older people or work with them, you know how many of them long for companionship and connection. The crooks know this, and feign interest in the elder's well-being and family in order to lower the elder's resistance to their inevitable request for personal information or money. This dynamic bears a chilling resemblance to the "grooming" phenomenon in child sex abuse cases, in that the elder, like the child victim, is singled out for special treatment intended to lower their guard.

At the same time, the senior victim is silently answering a series of questions within themselves about the person who is about to rip them off. In hypnosis we call this a *yes set*. In scamming it sets up the destructive delusional belief system through building rapport. A personal favorite author and trainer of mine in the fields of psychology and hypnosis, Dr. Michael Yapko, describes it this way in his book *Trancework*:

> "A yes set on the part of the client is a patterned response of accepting—in essence saying yes to—the suggestions you provide." (p 282)

The criminal makes a series of subtle, non-obvious suggestions creating a destructive illusion of themselves as a nice, kind, caring person who only wants the best for the victim. These suggestions are rife with distorted, magical thinking that skews everything the way the perpetrator wants it. When I train other mental health professionals about yes sets, I do an exercise with them in which I instruct a volunteer to simply say yes to questions like these:

"Is this a friendly, nice person?"

"Do they seem to like me?"

"Do they want to help me?"

"Do they want to give me something to make my life easier?"

"Do they have an easy solution to a problem I have?"

"Do they know what they are talking about?"

"Do they reassure me when I ask a question?"

"Can I trust them?"

"Will I do what they ask?" (The process moves to active manipulation here.)

This exercise demonstrates what goes on between the scammer and their victim.

A note about objections on the part of the victim: Manipulators want their victims to raise objections because objections provide useful emotional hooks for furthering rapport and building the destructive delusional belief system.

Now I will introduce you to the term I created to describe the essential linking of two interpersonal dynamics to hurt people. The term is *deceptulation*.

Deception means "deliberately misleading someone." This is different from misleading someone through incomplete or inaccurate information *without* malicious intent. In deception, you know what you're doing, and it isn't kind or helpful. You're seeking power over someone through lies and omission.

Manipulation is getting someone to do something you want, usually without their realizing it. It's the active part of a scam, in which the victim acts in accordance with the crook's lust for money or personal information.

I created the term *deceptulation* as a combination of *deception* and *manipulation* to reflect the mechanics of scam victimization. The scammers have to mislead the victim and get them to do what the criminal wants them to for the fraud to occur. They create a destructive delusional belief system in their victim to rip them off. Both deception and manipulation must be present for this to occur. The scammers are amazingly skillful at creating destructive belief systems, but I think we can all help scam-proof our elders with some easy-to-implement ideas.

In Section Three I discuss putting into action what we've learned about how the scammers do their dirty work so we can more effectively prevent the pain of scams and frauds.

SECTION THREE

Prevention: The Scam-Resistant Elder

Chapter 7
First Things

"The only defense against scammers is knowledge and skepticism."
— Steve Weisman, *The Truth about Avoiding Scams*

Consider the following stories:

- Apparently, in Russia and other countries, scam artists view Americans as rich and stupid, and they celebrate when they rip someone off.
- When I spoke with an investigator from a bank that issued several of Bill's credit cards, she told me this kind of crime is "rampant—if one group of criminals gets shut down, three more pop up in its place."
- The same investigator also told me that the US Secret Service, which has jurisdiction over matters like this, used to have a website just about Nigerian-type fraud, but had to shut it down "because there was too much demand" for help and information.

The people the criminals are hurting too much of the time are our own parents. It may be too late for your mom or dad. If it is, I am truly sorry. If it hasn't happened to them (or you) yet, read this chapter carefully. I intend that the ideas and tips help save you much pain, grief, and frustration.

Many authors and experts say it is impossible to totally prevent fraud against the elderly. Unfortunately, I have to agree with them. People of all ages—and elderly people in particular—can easily fall prey to the dangerous combination of a friendly, honest-sounding con artist and their own personal desire to gain something for nothing. Sometimes a senior thinks they are helping some poor unfortunate soul, only to discover that they are a victim of fraud. Despite the odds against total prevention, I enjoy giving talks to elders and training them to be more fraud and scam resistant. If I can help even one senior and their family avoid the pain and destruction wrought by these crooks, I'm happy.

Bear in mind that the world of scams, frauds, and identity theft is always evolving. As law enforcement and others are catching on to the latest twist, the crooks are already coming up with a new one. What I share with you in this chapter is current as of the writing of this book, and I hope to provide you with some basic principles for prevention that will stand the test of time. Another way to stay abreast of this fast-changing world is to visit my blog at www.elderlyfraudrecoveryhelp.com.

Let's face it—the perpetrators are better at their job of hurting people than the majority of elders currently are at staying safe. Most people will never be able to tell just by talking with someone whether or not that person is a criminal out to steal from them. The crooks are incredibly skillful at reeling in their victims without revealing their actual motives. Virtually everyone I've spoken with (including Bill) said the scammers were "very friendly" and "seemed totally honest." So what can be done? Let's start with an overall philosophy.

I propose that caregivers of seniors **MUST** think proactively to effectively manage and minimize the risk of victimization. This is not a subject about which to be in denial. I have seen firsthand how urgently seniors, their families, and professionals want information and support to prevent fraud. They are eager to know how to defeat scammers and protect themselves! As with many things in life, effective prevention is *simple*, but not *easy*.

There are some important concepts that inform effective prevention efforts. The first is the difference between prevention and detection. Prevention means to keep something from occurring in the first place. Detection, on the other hand, means discovering the existence of something which is already happening. Both are important, and when we have a choice, prevention is always better.

The other concept to keep in mind is that of primary versus secondary prevention. While these terms are most often used in the practice of medicine, I think they apply to scam prevention as well. *Primary prevention* means a scam doesn't happen in the first place, while *secondary prevention* means preventing more damage in an already-existing scam situation through early detection. Secondary prevention is what early detection is all about, whether we're describing a medical condition or fraud victimization. If you can't completely avoid a fraud or scam, at least limit the damage by catching it early.

First Things First: Does Your Parent Have Early Stage Cognitive Impairment?

Dr. Daniel Amen, on his website www.amenclinics.com, describes some recent studies showing that decision-making and financial skills are among the earliest faculties to decline—some two to three years before other symptoms of cognitive impairment become noticeable. As much as none of us wants to hear that news, it's better to know now rather than later. Your parent's doctor can determine if one of the new drugs that sometimes slow the progression of Alzheimer's disease might be helpful if your parent is having trouble with decision-making and/or financial tasks.

As family members or professionals work their way through the many tasks of handling the aftermath of a scam, I recommend they consider having the elderly victim tested for signs of Alzheimer's disease or other forms of dementia. If the victim's brain isn't working correctly, it changes how to proceed. As mentioned in Chapter 4, the Eight-Item Informant Interview to Differentiate Aging and Dementia©, or AD8, is a brief, easy-to-give screening test that may actually catch more early stage dementia than the standard Mini-Mental State Examination© (MMSE).

In a recent study, researchers at Washington University in St. Louis wanted to determine which of the two dementia screening tests worked better. They found that the AD8, in which a family member or close friend (the *informant*) answers the questions about the senior, more accurately helped diagnose early stage dementia. The MMSE, which is given by a healthcare worker, proved less reliable.

I think the AD8 also has a place in preventing frauds and scams against the elderly. Answers from a family member, close friend, case manager, or other care team partner who knows the senior well may better indicate the risk of being victimized than the MMSE. The AD8 identifies impairment that would reduce an elder's ability to recognize and respond effectively to a potential scam. You'll find the link for the AD8 in the resources in in the appendix of this book. Please note that the AD8 alone is not conclusive; a stronger assessment includes some sort of performance-based test administered by a trained professional, such as the MMSE or the Saint Louis University Mental Status Exam. As always, I recommend your parent be thoroughly evaluated by a qualified physician.

Scam Prevention at Different Levels of Cognitive Impairment

If you suspect your parent has some level of cognitive impairment, this section can help you protect your mom or dad based on the progression of their illness. I base the following recommendations on AD8 scores and suggest actions to take at each level of impairment. Every elder's situation is different, and flexibility is called for in setting up your plan. Each successive recommendation builds on the earlier ones.

Scam Prevention at a Mild Level of Cognitive Impairment (AD8 Scores of 2-4)

If your parent does have early dementia, prevention becomes vital. Consider respectfully taking steps to either limit the ability of outsiders to contact your parent, or closely monitor their contacts, including watching their accounts and credit reports carefully. In my presentations to families I call this "building the wall."

An important first step in this process is cleaning up any old relationship pain you may have with your parent. Most of us emerge from childhood with varying degrees of issues with our parents, even if we had great parents. Take the time to address these in some form if you possibly can so they do not impede your ability to help your parent in their time of increasing vulnerability. Pay special attention to any old pain that gets in the way of your supporting their ongoing needs for control and autonomy. You are going to need to leverage the relationship with your mom or dad in order to collaborate with them on building the protective wall between them and the criminals.

Here are some specific prevention recommendations, many of which can be helpful for people with normal cognitive function, too:

- Carefully consider having your parent grant you power of attorney. Definitely get the best legal advice you can find, and have the lawyer craft the document for maximum protection of your parent. Have a trusted third party review the actions and decisions granted to you in the document.

- Conduct "scam drills," which I will introduce in Chapter 8.

- Ask your parent regularly if anyone has asked them for money in any form, or if they have any new payments or bills they either didn't ask for, don't understand, or don't want.

- Make sure your parent has caller ID, so you can check it periodically for repeated calls from unknown numbers, especially those with foreign area codes.

- Set up a notification plan with banks, brokerages, and credit card companies so they have permission to sound the alarm about a possible fraud. As I was gathering the pertinent information for Steps 1 and 2 of my situation with Bill, I found out that the tellers at his credit union had suspected that something was amiss. They told me he had been coming into the branch more frequently than usual and withdrawing more and more money. One teller had even asked him if everything was OK, and Bill had said it was. If we had had a plan in place for the people at the bank to inform me about what was happening, we probably could have limited Bill's victimization earlier. You may be able to set this up through a power of attorney granting the bank officials permission to contact you should suspicions arise. Be aware, however, that recently there have been articles about some banks refusing to accept certain powers of attorney. As always, check with the institution and a qualified elder law attorney in your area for specifics.

- Consider banning your parent from money wiring services. For more about this, see Chapter 2.

- Watch for evasiveness on the part of your parent about money, a caregiver, a home repair worker, or anything else. They may express anger or agitation with you for asking. You presumably know your parent well and can tell if something is just not right or doesn't add up. Trust this sense, and check it out.

- Monitor your parent's home or property for fraudulent activity. There is a website called www.propertyfraudalert.com at which you can register your parent's property and an email address so that if anyone files a lien or other instrument against your parent's house you will be notified by email. Not all counties participate in the system yet, but if yours does, it's worth setting this up. The FBI calls property fraud one of the fastest growing crimes.

- With your parent's permission if possible, place a credit freeze on their accounts with each of the credit reporting agencies. A credit freeze stops access to your parent's credit reports and shuts down *new account fraud*, in which the crooks create a new account in your parent's name without their knowledge. Here's how to do it:

Requesting a Credit Freeze (or Security Freeze)

The preferred method of establishing a credit freeze seems to be by mail, although I've included the information below for freezing accounts online.

A customer requesting a freeze receives a personal identification number and/or password to use when changing the status of the freeze (e.g. temporary lifting or permanent removal). I recommend locking up such numbers/passwords with other crucial personal information.

With your letters to the three credit reporting agencies, you must send proof of your parent's identity and residence as follows:

One item to validate ID, such as:

- Valid driver's license
- Social Security card
- Pay stub
- W2 form

- 1099 form
- Court documents for legal name change
- Birth certificate
- Passport
- Marriage certificate
- Divorce decree
- State ID
- Military ID

AND two items to validate their address, such as:

- Valid driver's license
- Utility bill with the correct current address (gas, water, cable, residential phone bill)
- Cell phone bill
- Pay stub
- W2 form
- 1099 form
- Rental lease agreement/house deed
- Mortgage statement
- Bank statement
- State ID
- If your parent has recently moved, send a photocopy of their change of address card for their state driver's license or ID card.

Special Note: Always send items certified mail, return receipt requested.

Here is the contact information for the three credit reporting agencies:

Equifax
Security Freeze
PO Box 105788
Atlanta, GA 30348

Online:
https://www.freeze.equifax.com/Freeze/jsp/SFF_PersonalIDInfo.jsp

To check on applicable fees:
https://help.equifax.com/app/answers/detail/a_id/75/search/1

TransUnion Security Freeze
PO Box 6790
Fullerton, CA 92834-6790

Online:
https://annualcreditreport.transunion.com/fa/securityFreeze/landing

To check on fees:
http://www.transunion.com/corporate/personal/
fraudIdentityTheft/fraudPrevention/securityFreezeTable.page

Experian Security Freeze
PO Box 9554
Allen, TX 75013

Online: https://www.experian.com/freeze/center.html

To check on fees:
http://www.experian.com/consumer/security_freeze.html
then check drop-down menu at bottom for your state.

There are some important disadvantages to consider regarding credit freezes:

- It's important to plan ahead to temporarily suspend the credit freeze if your parent will be opening a new account or applying for a new loan such as a new car loan. Since many seniors don't use credit very often, this may not be a big disadvantage for your parent.
- It costs a non-victim anywhere from $5-$20 to both place and remove a credit freeze (victims of identity theft are not

charged a fee). If your parent accesses credit frequently, this can get expensive.

- You must place and lift a credit freeze with each credit agency, while you only have to contact one agency to place a fraud alert (discussed below) with all three.
- A credit freeze doesn't work as well as a fraud alert to prevent fraud involving existing accounts.

Consider your parent's individual situation and choose accordingly.

You can also place a fraud alert on your parent's accounts even if they haven't yet been a victim of a crime. Denis G. Kelly, author of the book *The Official Identity Theft Prevention Handbook*, proposes that taking this step may be even more effective than a credit freeze. This is because it makes creditors take an extra step to verify your parent's identity when your parent applies for new credit or to increase a credit limit on an existing account. You can have the creditor call you at the phone number you provide for verification when such a request is made. This shuts down new account fraud, but without the additional costs of placing and removing credit freezes. Alerts are free, but a downside of this approach is that your parent or you must remember to renew the fraud alert every 90 days. Here's the information for placing a fraud alert:

Equifax:

877-576-5734

https://www.alerts.equifax.com/AutoFraud_Online/jsp/fraudAlert.jsp

Experian:

888-397-3742

www.experian.com/fraud

TransUnion:

800-680-7289

www.transunion.com

Scam Prevention Ideas at a Moderate Level of Cognitive Impairment (AD8 Scores of 4-6)

Remember that the actions at this level are in addition to those for a mild level of cognitive impairment.

- Restricting the number of credit cards your parent holds may not go over well with them, and it may not be possible for everyone, but look long and hard at how many cards your parent holds. Get rid of all but a couple. I'm not suggesting you close the accounts, because that will lower your parent's credit score. But lock up the cards and documents in a safe deposit box or similar secure location. Experts suggest using each card once or twice a year to keep it in good standing. My mother, who was generally very astute financially, liked to collect credit cards; now I see this odd little quirk as loading the gun which was pointed directly at Bill's financial well-being after her passing.
- While we're on the subject of plastic, you may decide that debit cards, with their fewer protections, aren't a good idea for your parent. With a credit card, you have a chance to dispute a charge when the statement arrives or when you check the account online. Payees receive funds from debit card transactions very quickly, often immediately. They work like electronic checks. When a thief uses your parent's debit card number, potential losses go up with every passing day that you don't catch the problem. And a thief can use a debit card online or over the phone without having possession of the card or the PIN.

- Make sure you call your parent's financial institutions and credit card companies and have them stop sending convenience checks. Unless you opt out, they send periodic mailings with these checks enclosed—pre-printed with your parent's information, including account numbers. They are often sent with account statements as well, and if you don't look through the entire statement, you may not even realize the risk of leaving them out in your "bills to pay" pile. Convenience checks are supposed to make it easy to make a purchase, get cash, or transfer a credit card balance from another card. I think they are ticking time bombs; someone can steal them and use them quite easily, and crooks can coach your parent on using them to get cash to wire out of the country.
- Be sure to put valuables, car titles, and deeds in a safe deposit box or other secure storage if you haven't already done so. Scammers have been known to coach seniors on selling or pawning these items.
- Remove as much of your parent's information from the internet as you can. I cover this next:

Removing Your Parent's Information from the Internet

Googling your parent's name is a good first step to see what the world (including the scammers) has access to. Prepare to be surprised and dismayed at the personal information out there. When I checked on Bill's information, I found all of his addresses from the last 30 years or more, his phone numbers, his age, and the names of his relatives. For an additional charge you can find out the value of someone's home, names of neighbors, tax liens, and criminal records. It seems as if there really is no more privacy!

There are, at last count, over 15 major websites which may contain personal information about your parent. Public records such as property ownership can be found on government websites such as those for the county or city in which your mom or dad lives.

Blocking all this access is a tall order, and many authors and experts in the field of privacy rights say it's probably impossible to remove everything. You can, however, make a start by working to remove your parent's information from two of the biggest sources of private information for other websites, Intelius and Acxiom. **Contact these sites directly.** Here is the contact information:

Intelius:

http://www.intelius.com/privacy.php

Acxiom:

http://www.acxiom.com/about_us/privacy/consumer_information/opt_out_request_form/Pages/Opt-OutRequestForm.aspx

877-774-2094, option 5

Most sites allow you to remove data like address, phone number, and Social Security number. Each company has a different method, so be sure to read their webpages carefully and follow their respective procedures. Note that they will want you to provide personal information to prove that you are authorized to remove your parent's information, such as a copy of their driver's license or state-issued identification card.

Scam Prevention at a High Level of Cognitive Impairment (AD8 Scores of 6-8)

Once again, complete all the actions for the mild and moderate levels of cognitive impairment, plus the recommendations in this section. Remember to get a thorough medical evaluation to confirm any diagnosis.

At this level, it is time to look at actions such as establishing trusts, guardianship, and/or conservatorship. *Guardianship* is a formal, legal designation of someone who is responsible for the care and custody of a person unable to care for themselves, while *conservatorship* is a court appointment of someone to manage the financial resources of a person who is unable to do this for themselves. Taking such a step is a difficult decision, but it may be the best course for safeguarding your seriously impaired mom or dad. Great legal advice is vital anytime you are working with your parent's financial and legal affairs; it is especially crucial at this stage of their life.

Unfortunately, our elderly parents struggling with cognitive impairment are particularly vulnerable to the types of victimization I've covered in this chapter. Because the scammers lack conscience and/or play mind games with themselves about hurting others, our job is to "build a wall" between our parents and the crooks to the extent possible. Preventing frauds and scams is hard, but recovery is always harder and more painful.

Chapter 8

Unmet Needs, the Five FLAGS, and Scam Drills

"We become that which we practice most."

—Dr. Greg Lester

In the last chapter I introduced recommendations for fraud and scam prevention when your parent has cognitive impairment. Now we are going to take a further look at prevention and some next steps.

Consider Your Parent's Unmet Needs

In your assessment, you want to pay attention to your parent's *unmet needs,* which play a role in how the crooks get them to part with their money, personal information, and well-being. Unmet needs can change over time, and sometimes quite suddenly, as in the death of a spouse. How well do you know what's going on in your parent's life? For instance, how familiar are you with your parent's money issues? Was your father a tightwad, except in regard to home repairs? Did your mother want so much to help a family member or friend that she would do without to help that person? These kinds of issues, along with many others, can make your parent vulnerable to a scammer.

In the last chapter I talked about the five FLAGS as a way of beginning to think about your parent's unmet needs and vulnerabilities. Use my five FLAGS questionnaire to help you assess your parent's vulnerabilities:

The Five FLAGS Questionnaire

This questionnaire is a simple way for you to quickly assess your parent's potential for being victimized in a scam based on Fear, Loneliness, Anger, Greed, and Sympathy (the F.L.A.G.S.), plus a few other risk factors. The more yeses you mark, the greater the risk.

Y   N

____ ____ 1. My parent seems more fearful lately about their money and financial well-being.

____ ____ 2. My parent lives on a particularly tight income.

____ ____ 3. My parent sounds overwhelmed much of the time.

____ ____ 4. I think of my parent as a nervous person.

____ ____ 5. My parent spends much of their time alone.

____ ____ 6. My parent lives more than an hour's drive from close family members.

____ ____ 7. My parent has always been a "people person."

____ ____ 8. I believe my parent is lonely.

____ ____ 9. My parent has been prone to anger outbursts all their life.

____ ____ 10. My parent is angrier than usual recently.

____ ____ 11. My parent has always been critical of others.

____ ____ 12. I see my parent as bitter or resentful.

___ ___ 13. My parent has been a gambler, or has had a history of gambling addiction.

___ ___ 14. My parent loves to get a good deal.

___ ___ 15. My parent has always been eager to make money.

___ ___ 16. My parent has had problems with overspending.

___ ___ 17. My parent has fallen for sob stories in the past.

___ ___ 18. My parent will help anyone, even if my parent has to sacrifice to do so.

___ ___ 19. My parent seems to have a great concern for less fortunate people.

___ ___ 20. My parent has an overly trusting nature.

___ ___ 21. My parent's mother or father had a gambling addiction.

___ ___ 22. My parent has been ripped off or defrauded before.

___ ___ 23. My parent has been a victim of domestic violence, assault, or another traumatic event.

Your next step is to help your parent address the unmet needs you identified in the questionnaire. This may not be possible for every need, but at least now you know more about where your mom or dad may be at risk. Follow up by working out a plan to help them stay safe by conducting scam prevention education, or what I call "scam drills." (You can download my Guide to Scam Drills, which includes a 12-month scam drill plan, from my website www. elderlyfraudrecoveryhelp.com.) The more you tailor the drills to your parent's vulnerabilities as revealed in the questionnaire above, the greater the likelihood your parent will be able to avoid scam victimization.

A Basic Philosophy for Scam Prevention

I was talking to a good friend of mine recently about this book and my mission to help people whose parents have been scammed. She told me about a great quote she heard years ago from the magician Penn Jillette (of Penn and Teller fame), which captures the core of scam prevention. I have not been able to track down his exact words, so with apologies to Mr. Jillette, here is the idea:

"Never let yourself be chosen. Always do the choosing."

Our parents get excited when they have been "chosen" for some great offer or incredible prize. What is really happening is they have become a "mark," or next victim, of a scam artist. This is what happened to Bill, my stepfather. The crooks told him he had won third prize in the Publisher's Clearing House Sweepstakes, BUT he needed to send them money for fees, etc. That is how the fraud began.

When a person chooses with whom they do business, they can check them out online with the Better Business Bureau (BBB) or with their state attorney general. I further recommend asking friends and family what they know about the organization or individual. The common term for this today is *due diligence*. If they do not check out OK, or you cannot find any information, it is probably best to steer clear.

Choosing with whom to do business carries over to donations to charities as well. Elders are frequent targets for both fraudulent and genuine charities, so it's critical to warn them to watch out for "sound alike" charities, whose names are so similar to well-known charities that it's hard to tell that they are fraudulent.

Another thing to remember is that if a legitimate charity uses a telemarketing firm to make fundraising calls, often a very small percentage of the donation actually goes to the charity. For example, if your parent gives $100 to a telemarketing firm calling on behalf of the ASPCA, the telemarketing company may keep $80 for their fee, leaving only $20 for the worthy cause. Tell your parent that they should research a charity through watchdog sites such as www. charitynavigator.org or www.guidestar.org before donating.

As a police officer friend of mine also recommends, encourage your mom or dad to never donate over the phone, but instead make a direct donation to their local charity.

Penn Jillette's idea struck me with its simple clarity. To prevent our parents (and ourselves) from being ripped off, remind them often of this bit of wisdom:

"Never let yourself be chosen. Always do the choosing."

What Bill's Story Teaches Us about Prevention

After the dust settled a bit following the scam discovery, I asked Bill what he remembered about how the scammers might have gotten his name and phone number. He said he thought he had filled out a form for a company that offered to help with winning sweepstakes and the like. He recalled someone calling him, too, which got the scams going. What this suggests for prevention is to warn your parent, repeatedly and in multiple ways, never to give out personal information to a stranger or new contact without consulting you or someone else they trust. This would have to include, in my opinion, your parent's name and mailing address.

Is this extreme? Maybe. However, when weighing security against freedom, consider your parent's risk factors from this chapter and at least give it some thought. I thought I had handled this with Bill, having mentioned to him about never wiring money or paying for a prize. As I reflected further, I realized I hadn't said anything about this for over a year before the scams. Learn from my mistake; do a regular reminder – a scam drill – with your parent.

Conducting a Monthly Scam Drill

I was a flight attendant for a major airline for 18 years. While it definitely wasn't as glamorous as some people think, I learned a great deal in that time. Oddly enough, one of the most important things I learned was about the value of *practicing* safety procedures.

We had frequent safety briefings to review what to do in an emergency, and every year we went to the training center to practice opening the emergency doors and deploying the slides and other safety equipment. We drilled until it became second nature for us. While I was never in an emergency evacuation, a friend of mine who experienced an emergency said our training kicked in, and everyone knew exactly what to do.

So what does this have to do with preventing elderly people from getting ripped off? As one of my favorite trainers, Dr. Greg Lester, says, "We *become* that which we *practice most.*" To that end, I believe we can raise and support our elders' emotional intelligence and increase their scam resistance by conducting monthly scam drills with them.

The crooks start probing for vulnerabilities in their victims during the first contact. Raising seniors' emotional intelligence includes making them aware of their own vulnerabilities and educating them about the deceptiveness of con artists. Our parents need to be aware that scammers "sound so nice" on the phone, and that they target victims in person and in print. If we regularly practice with a senior the correct skills, they are much less likely to fall victim to criminals.

Scams and frauds take many forms, and criminals are always adapting their methods and approaches. This is why I recommend scam drills and practicing a core set of skills embodied in three Rs:

- Recognizing
- Responding
- Reaching Out

Recognizing a Scam

Recognizing a scam includes:

- Recognizing the *vulnerabilities* the scammer is trying to use against your parent. This may involve one or more of the five FLAGS, or some form of cognitive distortion or magical thinking.
- Recognizing the *tactics* the scammer is using to manipulate your parent into doing what the scammer wants them to do. These tactics include phony urgency and conveying that the deal is rare and your parent is unique in having the opportunity to cash in on it, which show up in most kinds of scams and frauds.
- Recognizing the presence of an attempted scam based on *what the con artist is trying to get your parent to do.*

A major part of prevention is practicing appropriate critical thinking skills, also known as healthy skepticism. But what does this mean, exactly? In my talks to seniors and professionals I speak about ten dead giveaways for scams:

1. **The scammer chooses you in any way.**

2. **The scammer tells you to keep secret the actions they are asking you to carry out.**

3. **The scammer is very nice or charming.**

4. **The scammer asks for money or personal information, especially money in any form for a prize of some kind.**

5. **The scammer tells some sort of sob story or requests help.**

6. **The scammer employs urgency, immediacy, or forcefulness ("You must do this *now!*").**

7. "Too good to be true" claims which elicit emotions such as greed, excitement, relief, and gratitude, and reactions such as "It's only a few bucks; why not take a chance?"

8. The scammer asks you to wire or receive money, especially to or from someone you do not know.

9. The scammer asks you to go with them somewhere.

10. The scammer asks to come into your home to use the phone, go to the bathroom, etc.

Recognizing these dead giveaways forms the cornerstone for knowing you are about to become a victim of a scam.

Responding

By educating your parent about scams and practicing scam drills, you empower them to respond firmly, decisively, and quickly should they suspect a scammer is at work. You are enabling your parent to *set and keep boundaries in order to stay safe.*

Spend time teaching your parent how to evaluate a scammer's verbal pitch, written offer, or email plea. Emphasize that it is important to determine what the scammer is asking them to do. Tell them to THINK FIRST any time someone asks them for money, personal information, or to be a part of some activity. This automatically slows down the behavioral chain that leads to big problems. Ideally you will practice the scam prevention mindset and actions with your parent, and they will remember to END THE CONTACT IMMEDIATELY.

Tell your parent that if they are not sure something is a scam to call you or someone they know and trust to check out the company, organization, or claim. Practice with your elder how to resist the phony urgency the scammers use to stoke anxiety and make your parent give them money.

Also—and this is especially critical—repeatedly emphasize to never let how nice the person is influence their actions. Here are some tips for how to say no to a nice person:

- Actually say "No."
- Be *firm* and *kind.* By being firm, you establish clear boundaries regarding contact with the potential scammer and what they are trying to get you to do. Less is always better when it comes to contact with scammers.
- While scammers don't really deserve to have someone treat them kindly, being polite allows you to feel better about setting the boundary. Most people don't want to be mean to anyone, even a scammer. Being kind to someone who is trying to rip you off allows you to feel that you are not stooping to a lower level just because you are faced with a criminal. If you want to be nasty to a scammer, go right ahead! As long as you don't fall for the phony pitch and give the crook any money or personal information, let 'em have it!

Here are some examples of ways to say no to a nice person:

"I'm sorry, I can't talk right now." (Close the door or hang up the phone immediately.)

"I'll have to talk to my son/daughter first." (Close the door or hang up the phone immediately.)

"No thank you." (Close the door or hang up the phone immediately.)

"I'm not interested. Thank you anyway." (Close the door or hang up the phone immediately.)

Notice that each suggestion includes ending the contact immediately after the statement. This principle holds true for an even more sinister method some scammers have been using lately: the scam based on intimidation. I've heard and read an increasing number of stories about criminals becoming belligerent and intimidating on the phone. Sometimes they even threaten to hurt the elder or their family. Be sure to notify the police if this happens. If the criminal on the line is being nasty and/or attempting to coerce your parent into doing what they want them to, it's especially important to coach your parent to hang up quickly. Sometimes the criminal will turn nasty after seeming "so nice" to increase the confusion and fear to better manipulate the victim. Remember, con artists will use anything and everything to hook your parent and keep them on the line. Remind your mom or dad that this step—ending the contact—is the most vital of all.

What about In-Person Scams?

From time to time a story will appear in the media about an elderly person who becomes the victim of a scam when they are shopping or away from home. A classic example of this is the so-called "pigeon drop." This is when a crook approaches their victim in public and entices them to join in a scheme to make money, promising the victim a larger cash reward in exchange for fronting the criminals some cash. The next thing the victim knows, the crooks have switched the cash for a worthless stack of bill-sized paper and disappear with the money, leaving the victim with nothing.

A story appeared in my local newspaper as I was writing this section of the book that illustrates how this scam works. Two men approached an 89-year-old gentleman in front of a grocery store and told him they wanted him to withdraw $5,000 from his bank to get in on a deal to split $100,000 supposedly coming from a foreign country. They all drove to a restaurant and the criminals led him to believe that his money was wrapped in a cloth that they left in his car before they went into the restaurant to make the call to their connection. When they didn't come back, the victim found that they had switched his $5,000 for a bunch of torn-up newspaper.

Thankfully, an alert off-duty police officer who had taken a report from a victim of the same crime the day before that saw two men who matched the suspects' descriptions, picked up on what was happening, and saved someone from being ripped off in the same way the next day.

Recognizing this type of scam means catching several of the ten dead giveaways: The scammers *chose* the person, they presented a *"too good to be true"* situation, they were probably *nice*, and they played up *urgency*.

Another type of in-person scam to watch out for is when someone asks your parent if they can come into their house to use the phone, go to the bathroom, or for some other seemingly innocuous reason. Police trainers who speak to officers about scams against the elderly say that if the crook gets in the victim's home, IT'S OVER—meaning the elder is going to be ripped off in some way. Often the thief is looking for valuables, prescription drugs, or personal information such as credit cards or a Social Security number. I cannot emphasize enough to seniors to NEVER let someone they do not know into their home.

Reaching Out

An expert on personality disorders told me that psychologists who treat these disorders work in teams to prevent being taken in by the patients' cons and manipulations. We should also work in teams with our parents, and encourage them to work with other trusted people as well. After all, especially in the crazy world of (probably psychopathic) scammers, the more trusted or at least impartial eyes looking at a potential scam, the better.

We and our trusted family and care team members are a kind of "survival herd" looking out for our vulnerable parents. Reaching out, therefore, means coaching our elder loved ones to involve family, care team members, community resources, and law enforcement when a scam is suspected or discovered. Teach your parent to ask for support and help in verifying the claims or validity of a questionable offer, and to ask other people who are at least somewhat likely to be trustworthy for their opinion or help, including asking a store security guard or manager for help if they're accosted in a parking lot.

Another dimension of reaching out involves having your parent tell their friends and neighbors about encounters with likely scam situations. When your mom or dad responds successfully to a fraud that comes their way, they have a reason to feel good about themselves. This isn't about bragging, it's about feeling a sense of validation for their efforts to stay safe. Spreading the word can help your loved one feel good about helping others stay safe, too. Knowledge in this case is both power and protection.

You can, of course, modify scam drills as you see fit for your situation. If you feel your parent is already pretty savvy about these things, maybe you will want to do the scam drill with them every other month or quarterly instead of monthly. I encourage you to read up on the latest scams and throw your parent a new twist from time to time.

Make scam drills as fun and lighthearted as possible. Frauds and scams are serious business, but working to defeat scammers and con artists can be done in a spirit of playing a game or learning something useful. Again, use your knowledge of your own parent to guide your scam drill practice.

You can download my Guide to Scam Drills from my website at www.elderlyfraudrecoveryhelp.com. It includes a 12-month scam drill plan and other helpful hints.

Chapter 9

Preventing More Pain: Financial Abuse and Identity Theft

"The most important prevention tactic is to pay attention."
—Denis G. Kelly, *The Official Identity Theft Prevention Handbook*

Preventing Financial Abuse by Family Members and Caregivers

These kinds of situations are excruciatingly painful and difficult. The sense of betrayal, violation, anger, loss, and sadness can be overwhelming for everyone touched by financial abuse of the elderly. Families can be torn apart, resulting in broken relationships and years of estrangement. There may also be irreparable damage to the victim(s), both financially and emotionally.

According to research from the National Criminal Justice Reporting Service, about 60 percent of financial abuse perpetrators were relatives of the victim—most often an adult child. It's sad to me that the very people who are supposed to be looking out for an elder in their time of need are often the ones exploiting them.

Include your parent in a family meeting to make an agreement about who will eventually look after them financially and physically.

Scammed

Hopefully you can hold this meeting before your parent experiences cognitive impairment. If your parent is already experiencing cognitive difficulties, find a counselor or other professional who can attend the meeting as well to provide professional assistance.

What to Watch For

It's mostly up to family, friends, and trusted others to watch for patterns that might indicate financial abuse. Here are some signs to watch for:

- Your parent has a new "best friend."
- Your parent becomes more socially isolated.
- Your parent seems reluctant to have contact with others unless their caregiver is present.
- Your parent's bills go unpaid when someone else is responsible for paying them.
- You notice missing property, large or unexplained withdrawals from bank accounts, or transfers between accounts.
- Your parent changes their financial institutions, advisors, or attorneys.
- Bank or brokerage statements and canceled checks no longer come to your parent's home. This could be a sign of account hijacking—when someone takes over the victim's accounts.
- You notice unfamiliar signatures on checks and other documents.
- Your parent changes their spending patterns, such as buying items they don't need or spending higher than normal amounts.
- Your parent makes cash-back transactions at grocery stores or the pharmacy. This may indicate *account dripping*, in which a thief takes a small amount of money many times, thinking no one will ever notice. According to police, it's also shockingly common for store employees to overcharge an unsuspecting

senior by $5 or $10 on a debit card transaction hoping they'll never notice. After the senior leaves, the employee pockets the overcharge.

- Your parent's lack of personal items such as clean clothes and grooming products.

In terms of prevention, each situation is different, so I can't suggest a simple formula beyond paying attention to changes in patterns and routines. A full discussion of this topic is beyond the scope of this book, nevertheless there are some general ideas to consider.

As I was working on this book, I talked to my own financial advisor about my interest in this subject, and he told me that the important take-away message from cases of financial abuse he was familiar with was "The more eyes on the money, the better." In other words, it is vital for trustworthy family members to set up strong monitoring and accountability practices for safeguarding their vulnerable elder's finances. Financial advisors talk about "layers of protection." This can mean your parent holding a joint bank account with one sibling and a different sibling or other trusted party receiving and monitoring the account statements.

Be extra careful with powers of attorney. Some professionals recommend against appointing a relative as the elder's agent. On the other hand, there are numerous examples of lawyers who have financially exploited elders via a power of attorney. Think about your parent's situation carefully. It might work to create a joint power of attorney with a trusted relative and a certified or licensed professional, or have someone monitor the designated agent. This is another time for good legal advice.

Some other ideas you may want to consider include:

- Requiring the co-signer on the bank account to provide regular accounting statements

- If you can't be your parent's agent, and don't trust anyone else, consider using a professional fiduciary. This is a person paid to make decisions for your parent about their money and investments, and to sign checks. They typically charge about $75 to $150 per hour, and you can ask your elder law attorney or accountant for a referral. You can also do an internet search under keywords such as "professional fiduciary New York City," for example.
- A less expensive option is to use a professional geriatric care manager to pay bills and deal with home repairs and the like. According to the National Association of Geriatric Care Managers (www.caremanager.org), 35 to 40 percent of their members perform this function. Fees are typically less than half of what a lawyer would charge.
- Create an inventory of your parent's personal property, especially valuable items, so you can tell if something goes missing. Some people even take pictures of their parent's rooms at home and note the location of important items. Be sure the photos have a time and date attached to them.

A big source of problems is your parent providing financial assistance and/or loans to family members. While most elders want to help out a struggling child or grandchild and find it gratifying, I encourage elders and their families to be very cautious about what they're getting into. I recommend entering into a written, legal agreement that spells out the details and ensures that your parent's reimbursement is the top priority. A neutral third party outside the family, like an attorney or geriatric care manager, should supervise adherence to the agreement.

I think it's also important to monitor each person who has access to your parent. Think about the person and their situation in terms of potential risks—things like financial problems, excessive debt, drug or alcohol abuse, overspending, and gambling addiction. That said, the more trustworthy eyes on your parent's money and property, the better.

Preventing Identity Theft

According to some experts, identity theft is the most common scam or fraud in the country. Javelin Strategy and Research stated in its 2012 Identity Fraud Report that approximately 11.6 million people of all ages were victims of identity theft in 2011 in the US, with elders counting for roughly 10 percent, or 1.16 million of them. This may significantly understate the problem because some victims never report it.

As a member of your parent's care team, you are in a unique position to be on guard for your parent and protect them from identity theft and other scams based on theft of personal information. Victimization often involves multiple problems with identity theft being just one part of the package. Prevention is vital for all types of scams, but perhaps even more so when it comes to identity theft because of the potential for greater damage.

I created a simple test for audiences I speak to which can help you gauge how safe your parent is (or isn't) from identity theft:

How Safe Are *YOU*?

Identity Theft Assessment Test

Please answer each question yes or no:

- I have a shredder and use it.
- I use different passwords for each account I have at financial institutions.
- My passwords contain a mix of characters.
- I have reviewed copies of my credit reports in the last year.
- I do not carry my Social Security number, birth certificate, or passport in my purse or wallet unless I need it for a special reason.

- I never reply to any email or phone call asking me for personal information, even if I know it is from my financial institution.
- I keep my personal files locked up at home or at my office.
- I never leave my purse or wallet in my car, even in the trunk.
- If a worker or housecleaner is coming over, I make sure my personal mail is locked out of sight.
- If I mail a bill payment, I always put it in a post office mail slot or mailbox.
- I check my bank account balances at least monthly.
- I carry no more than two credit cards with me.
- I always sign off from my financial institutions' websites before visiting a different website.
- I never use a public network for banking or paying bills.
- I have opted out of preapproved credit card offers and convenience checks.
- My home computer or network is secured or password-protected.
- I check my health insurance estimates of benefits (EOBs) for errors.
- I have registered my phone numbers on the do not call list.
- I reconcile or check my account statements within a week of receiving them.
- I have placed a credit freeze or fraud alert on my credit reports.
- I never use my driver's license as collateral or a security deposit when shopping.
- I have requested the "verify ID" option for my driver's license with my state motor vehicle agency (if available in my state).
- I have installed anti-virus and anti-spyware programs on my computer, and I keep them updated.
- I always take my credit card receipts with me and dispose of them securely after I buy something.
- I securely dispose of checks from accounts I close, and I make sure to pick up new checks at the bank rather than have them mailed to my house.

More yes answers means the safer you are from possible identity theft. Each "no" answer should become an item to correct as soon as possible. I discuss ideas from the test in the next section and suggest some more ways to help your parent stay safe from identity thieves.

The Basics of Identity Theft

First and foremost, be sure you clearly remember the difference between prevention and detection that I wrote about in Chapter 7. Based on how some companies market identity theft protection, there's a great deal of confusion about it. Denis G. Kelly's worthwhile book, *The Official Identity Theft Prevention Handbook*, helps clarify the important difference between identity theft prevention and detection:

"By definition, this strategy [prevention] entails tactics that avoid identity theft altogether... [detection] indicators [mean] your identity has been compromised." (location 575, Kindle edition)

Another important idea to keep in mind is the difference between *primary prevention* and *secondary prevention* (see Chapter 7). Recall that primary prevention means a scam doesn't happen in the first place, while secondary prevention means preventing more damage in an already-existing scam situation through early detection.

Primary Identity Theft Prevention

- If your parent doesn't have a shredder for sensitive documents, encourage them to get one right away and use it for anything that contains personally identifying information. In addition to the usual items to be shredded, remind them to shred utility and other bills. The most effective shredders are the "confetti" or "perforated" style.
- Verify subscription and utility bills to be sure they really belong to your parent.

- Be sure your parent shreds pre-approved credit card offers and convenience checks from credit card companies if they haven't yet opted out of them.
- Encourage your parent to not carry any government-issued documents with any personal information on them unless they need them for official business. This includes their Social Security card, birth certificate, and passport.
- Remind your parent from time to time to never give out <u>any</u> personal information of <u>any</u> kind over the phone or internet unless they initiated the call or contact and it is an organization they know and trust.
- Place a credit freeze or fraud alert (see Chapter 7).
- Encourage your parent to opt out of pre-approved credit card offers and convenience checks by calling 888-5-OPT-OUT (888-567-8688) or going to <u>www.optoutprescreen.com</u>. This simple step prevents an identity thief from taking out credit in your parent's name by diverting or stealing their mail.
- Suggest that your parent register with the do not call list if they haven't already done so: 888-382-1222 or <u>www.donotcall.gov</u>
- Verify that your parent has important papers locked up when home repair people or caregivers are due, especially their Social Security card; Medicare card (which, of course, have their SSN on them!); physician, bank, and credit card statements; and brokerage or other financial institutions' statements. This goes for checkbooks and blank checks, too.
- Keep close watch on repair people and home care providers when they visit. Ask your home care company in advance for the full names of the providers and any other information they can release about them, then check them out yourself on websites such as <u>www.criminalsearches.com</u>.
- Start and keep up a running visitors' log for everyone who enters your parent's home, including home care providers and

repair people. Have everyone provide the date and time they arrived and left in addition to their name.

- Be sure to report lost or stolen cards or other documents with personal information on them to the correct institution immediately. In addition to credit and debit cards, think health insurance cards, driver's license, and checkbooks.
- Ask banks, credit unions, and other financial institutions to place an additional layer of security protection on your parent's accounts. This is usually an extra password (in addition to the usual PIN) that someone has to provide to change a mailing address, set up a new account, or increase available credit. Check with your parent's respective institutions about this free, simple step.
- Encourage your parent to carry only one or two credit cards.
- Recommend that your parent never use their driver's license as a deposit when they are shopping for a car or other item.
- Remind your parent to reconcile and balance their bank and credit card statements as soon as possible, ideally within one week of receiving them.
- Have your parent take credit card receipts with them and bring them home to shred after verifying the charges on their statements.
- If your parent closes a checking account, be sure they shred the old checks and deposit slips right away.
- Make sure your parent uses only gel pens for writing checks and other personal information. When I talk to groups of seniors I always bring a supply to give away. These pens have special ink that prevents *check washing*—erasing details from checks and rewriting them. A good brand is the line from Uni-Ball.
- Mask the first five digits of your parent's Social Security number when you request copies of their credit reports. This significantly increases the level of security for a credit report. Simply request to have the first five digits masked.

- Make sure your parent has a locking mailbox or a mail slot in their front door. Traditional mailboxes with flags are a major way identity thieves steal mail to get account numbers and other important information. The flag tells thieves that your mail is in the box for the taking.
- Tell your parent to always put their outgoing mail with sensitive information in a mail collection slot at the post office or at one of the mailboxes on post office property.
- Remind your parent to have their mail stopped if they are going to be away. This is especially important if they still have an external mailbox.
- Trust your gut. If something sounds fishy, report it to the police or check with your state attorney general's office.

Secondary Identity Theft Prevention

These steps are a way to detect possible existing problems and limit further damage:

- Run a yearly check on your parent's credit reports via www.annualcreditreport.com. You can also call 877-322-8228. Go over them for errors and/or accounts that are not your parent's. Immediately report any errors or questionable accounts.
- Inform your parent about and help them watch for multiple addresses on their Social Security statements, which can indicate that someone is fraudulently receiving benefits under their name.
- Watch for any unusual patterns with your parent's mail. Look for bank and credit card statements that used to come but no longer seem to be coming. Identity thieves submit change of address requests to perpetrate their crimes. I recommend creating and using a mail calendar or log based on simple

tracking of when regular checks or bills arrive. Better yet, consider setting up automatic deposit for checks and online or automatic bill-pay services.

- Make a copy of all your parent's identification cards and documents, credit and debit cards, Social Security card, and health insurance card(s). Add to these copies the contact information to use in case of loss or theft. Put these in a secure but accessible location such as a fireproof lockbox. This is secondary prevention; if the worst happens, you'll have everything you need to work on recovery in one secure location and can save time in the crucial first hours after discovery of a problem.

Staying Secure Online

More and more seniors are getting online, especially for shopping. Here are some ideas to help them keep their identity secure while online:

- Tell your parent to only buy from merchants they know.
- Tell your parent to make sure a seller's website has either https:// in the web address or a small padlock icon in the lower right corner of the frame around the window.
- Tell your parent that if they receive an email or phone call from a bank or other financial institution or service provider telling them there's a problem with their account, it's likely a scam. They should never provide information in response to such a call and should always call the customer service number on the statement or the back of the card to verify whether such a call is legitimate.
- Tell your parent never to open emails from people they don't know, and that it's prudent to avoid downloading files from the internet unless they have verified the trustworthiness of the person or website the file is coming from.

- Help your parent install anti-virus and anti-spyware software on their computer, and be sure they keep them updated. They also need to have a firewall on their home wireless network if they have one, and it should be secure/password-protected. You may have to do this for them or hire someone to do it.
- Tell your parent never to access online banking or any other financial websites from a public network such as a coffee shop or library.
- If your parent gets a new computer, physically destroy the hard drive on the old one after transferring files. Erasing it is not good enough.
- Tell your parent not to put any personal information on social networking sites like Facebook, including their full name, full names of their children or grandchildren, address, or phone number. Tell them never to post that they're leaving town.

Medical Identity Theft

This is a serious problem that most children of elder parents know very little about. The existence of incorrect medical information due to identity theft is more than just inconvenient, it can be downright deadly. If an identity thief has different medical conditions than your parent, your mom or dad could receive unnecessary or incorrect treatment. An incorrect medical account is difficult to detect because it doesn't show up on credit reports until an account goes to collections.

In November of 2011, the Associated Press reported on the scope of data breaches in the healthcare industry during the prior two years. It's shocking to know that there were 364 reported incidents of data loss in the US involving nearly 18 million patients—"equivalent to the population of Florida," according to the authors of the original article on the website Boston.com. In addition, Javelin Strategy and Research reported there were 1.5 million medical identity theft victims in the US in 2010.

What can you do to prevent your parent from becoming a victim of medical identity theft? Here are some ideas:

Primary Medical Identity Theft Prevention

- Remind your parent to shred any health insurance related paperwork they no longer need, such as explanations of benefits (EOBs), physicians' statements, and prescription drug statements.
- Tell your parent to never give out personal health plan information to someone over the phone or internet unless your parent has initiated the contact and can verify the trustworthiness of the person they speak with.
- The US Federal Trade Commission recommends destroying the labels on prescription drug bottles and packages before discarding them.

Secondary Medical Identity Theft Prevention

- Go over explanations of benefits (EOBs) as soon as you can after they arrive. Verify names, dates, and procedures. Report any errors or discrepancies immediately.
- Review copies of your parent's medical records. This carries a high "pain in the butt" factor because you'll have to request a copy of each provider's records, but it is critically important because of the potential for life-threatening errors.
- Review annual summaries of benefits from your parent's health insurers.

For more guidance about identity theft prevention see Resources and Recommended Reading in the appendix.

Identity Theft Protection Services

I'm not a fan of most identity theft protection services. There are a few problems with almost all of them from my experience and research:

- They sell *prevention*, but actually provide *detection*.
- They often have mixed motives: making money by selling access to credit *and* providing "prevention."
- Most of what you pay them to do, you can do for yourself or your parent.

You may decide you don't have the time or want the hassle of dealing with prevention yourself, and you want to check into prevention services. Be careful that you and your parent are actually getting the prevention you're paying for and not just after-the-fact detection.

SECTION FOUR

Putting the Steps into Practice with Three Common Problems

Chapter 10
Recovering from Telemarketing Scams

"All deception in the course of life is indeed nothing else but a lie reduced to practice, and falsehood passing from words into things."

—Robert Southey

Aren't telemarketers annoying? You're right in the middle of dinner or the good part of a movie, and they call trying to sell you some dumb thing or seeking a donation. Even if you're on the government's do not call list, they still manage to bug you with phony sounding surveys and pleas for money. And don't even get me started about those political "robo-calls"!

These are examples of telemarketing—someone trying to connect with you via the telephone to sell something to you or get you to do something. It's a common way of doing business, and perhaps the most common way our elders get ripped off. Older people are frequently home during the day, and the criminals know this. They also know that our parents and other elder loved ones tend to be more polite than others because they were raised that way, and this ends up getting elders in trouble. Many elders I talk to are uncomfortable saying no to a pushy person, not to mention a nice person.

Some authors call telemarketing scams "getting mugged with a telephone." I think that's particularly apt. As I covered in my earlier chapter on the psychology of scamming, when a skilled psychofinancial predator interacts with a vulnerable senior, the senior usually ends up losing. Although every crime is different, here are some ideas for how to handle the mess left behind:

Step 1 for Telemarketing Scams

Discovery: A Quick Review of the Signs of Telemarketing Fraud

Naturally you want to be sure that a telemarketing scam or fraud is actually present. Here are some signs:

- Your parent receives an unusual number of calls from unknown people or phone numbers.
- Your parent is secretive or sneaky about such calls; they don't answer questions directly.
- You notice a different pattern in your parent's financial transactions, especially a large number of bank debits.
- Your parent asks you to help them get money orders.
- You notice unusual phone numbers on your parent's caller ID, either incoming or outgoing. Especially watch for Canadian and Caribbean area codes associated with scammers targeting elders in the US. (For links to area code maps for Canada and the Caribbean, see the appendix.)
- Your parent's phone bill is much higher than usual.
- Your parent tells you they've won a prize, lottery, or sweepstakes of some kind. (This is always a red light on your dashboard.)
- You notice or hear about a courier coming to your parent's house without a good reason.

If you notice any of the above signs, your parent is probably getting ripped off in a telemarketing scam. Here are your next steps:

Putting the Steps into Practice with Three Common Problems

Checklist for Step 1

Questions to ask:

___ "Has anyone threatened to hurt you or anyone close to you?"

If the answer is yes, NOTIFY THE POLICE.

___ "Did you give anyone you talked to personal information like account numbers, passwords, your Social Security number, or other identifying information?"

If the answer is yes, go directly to Step 2 and stop any potential bleeding. Call all financial institutions and put temporary freezes on all accounts. You will probably need power of attorney to do this. See also Chapter 12 on recovering from identity theft for more guidance.

Next Steps:

___ I have power of attorney.

___ List bank and credit union name(s), phone numbers, and account numbers here:

_____

_____

_____

_____

_____

___ Gather all credit cards and list credit card issuers' names, card numbers, and customer service phone numbers here:

_____

_____

_____

_____

(Note: Do your best to hold on to your parent's credit cards to prevent more losses if they used cash advances to fund the scam. Assure them this is only temporary.)

___ List name(s) and phone number(s) of your parent's stockbroker and other places your parent's investments are held here:

_____

_____

_____

Questions to ask:

___ "How much money did you give them (approximately)?" Write answer here:

_____

___ "How often have you spoken with or had contact with the people involved? Has this happened more than once?"

_____

___ "To whom was the money sent or given?" List all names here:

_____

_____

_____

_____

_____

___ "Did you ever receive money from someone you don't know and send it on to a different person?" If yes, write the name(s) here:

_____

_____

_____

__ "Which account(s) did you use to get cash to give to the people involved?" List them, with account numbers, here:

_____

_____

_____

__ "Did you get the money yourself, or did someone you spoke with get it from your account or credit card?" (Note: If your parent tells you someone else got the money from one of their accounts or credit cards, their personal information has been compromised. See the second question at the top of the checklist and call your parent's financial institutions NOW.)

__ "Can you show me any receipts, phone records, or other papers pertaining to what's happened?"

Tasks to be completed:

__ I have all the papers and receipts I can find that pertain to the crime(s) against my parent in one place.

__ I have started documenting all phone calls and conversations about the scam(s).

__ I have started a crime timeline (see Chapter 1).

__ I have clearly determined the type(s) of scam(s) affecting my parent.

__ I am backing up all fraud-related computer files weekly.

Step 2 for Telemarketing Scams

Protect Your Parent: Stop the Bleeding and Lock Down the Assets

When you suspect your parent is getting ripped off over the phone, it's critical to *end the contact now.* Contact by phone is the way scammers created the delusional, manipulative fog which is hurting your parent, so you have to deny them this access to your parent.

Remember that your parent may still believe the crooks are their friends or are "really nice people." Never underestimate the criminals' skills or your parent's capacity for denial. If your mom or dad still thinks the crooks are not what they are, review the section on denial in Chapter 1.

Another point to keep in mind is that each scam or fraud is unique, and your steps may vary. Stay in your best flexible problem-solving mode and ask for help if you need it.

Checklist for Step 2

___ Call your parent's financial institutions. Inform them about what's happened and ask them to place a fraud alert on the accounts. (Note: Skip this task if completed in Step 1.)

___Call the three credit reporting agencies and place a fraud alert on your parent's accounts:

___ Experian

___ TransUnion

___ Equifax

___ I have a copy of my parent's credit reports from all three credit reporting agencies. (www.annualcreditreport.com)

___ I have changed my parent's phone numbers (remember to write down the new number(s) for your parent and notify friends, family, doctors, and the pharmacy).

___ I have explained reloading to my parent and warned them not to talk about the situation to anyone they don't know. I have requested that my parent refer all calls about the scam to me. Alternatively, I have forwarded my parent's phone to my cell phone or home phone.

___ I have changed my parent's email address if the scam involved any email contact with the criminals (remember to write down the new address for your parent and notify the people in their address book).

___ I have banned my parent from Western Union, MoneyGram, and other local money wiring companies if the scam involved wiring money.

___ We have filed a police report.

___ We have filed a complaint with the state attorney general.

___ We have filed a complaint with the FTC.

___ I have notified my parent's primary care doctor

Step 3 for Telemarketing Scams

Recovery: Make Your Recovery Plan

Checklist for Step 3

___ I have a reasonably accurate amount of the total loss my parent has incurred.

___ I have completed an updated spending plan for my parent.

___ I have made contact with the investigations department of my parent's financial institution(s) (as applicable).

___ I have contacted a financial adviser and made an appointment to discuss options for restoring lost cash.

___ I have spoken with my parent's tax preparer and informed them about the losses.

___ I have acquired IRS Publication 547 and have a copy of a police report or attorney general complaint to file with their taxes. (http://www.irs.gov/pub/irs-pdf/p547.pdf)

___ My parent has had a thorough medical checkup and mental status exam.

___ I am monitoring my parent's mail.

___ I am encouraging and helping my parent enhance their quality of life.

Chapter 11
Recovering from Home Repair Rip-offs

"Truth lives on in the midst of deception."

—Friedrich von Schiller

Did you know that Americans spend over $200 billion a year on home remodeling and repair? Did you know that home remodeling and repair contractors ranked just behind car salespeople and auto mechanics for the most consumer complaints, according to the Council of Better Business Bureaus? I frequently hear from elders or their family members about a home repair contractor who has taken the money but hasn't performed the work, and now the contractor won't return calls or emails.

Elderly people are frequently victims of home repair scams for several reasons:

- They are often home during the day when crooked contractors are out trolling neighborhoods where elderly people live looking for "marks" (victims).
- They are not as physically capable of keeping up with routine and special maintenance, and often find it overwhelming or scary.
- They may not be informed enough about house maintenance needs or problems, making them susceptible to a fast-talking con artist.

- They often live in older homes that need more repairs.
- They may live in paid-for homes or have a great deal of equity built up in them.

When my parents were ripped off in the mid-'90s by a home repair scammer, I called a consulting engineer. An engineer can come to your parent's house and assess what was done versus what needed to be done. He told me about the poor job the crook had done on the original "problem" (cracks in the mortar of an all-brick home), and about the way the fraudster had botched the job of putting in a new lateral line from the house to the sanitary sewer.

I have since learned that you can get similar advice from a home inspector. The important thing is to get good, solid advice about what you need to do to handle the aftermath of a home repair fraud, unless you happen to have this knowledge yourself. With potential problems involving safety, code violations, and thousands of dollars, recovery from these kinds of crimes requires expert information.

In addition to the kind of home repair scam in which elderly people pay exorbitant fees for needless or exaggerated repairs, sometimes they fall prey to home improvement loan scams. This is the double whammy; not only may they not really need the repairs, but the crooks arrange financing using the home as security for the dubious loan. If the victim fails to repay the loan, they can lose their home.

The steps for dealing with a home repair scam include some different elements because it involves a large physical asset. You have to make sure the house is safe to live in and meets all relevant building and fire codes.

Step 1 for Home Repair Rip-offs

Discovery: Signs of Home Repair Fraud

- Your parent says a person stopped by the house and offered to fix something for them, especially if the contractor claimed the repairs were urgent or needed to correct a code violation. They may also claim to have materials left over from another job, or just did an "inspection" on your parent's house.

- A crook might exploit your parent by claiming that your parent called them but "must have forgotten." Listen for any story like this from your mom or dad.

- Your parent says someone called them on the phone or came to the door and offered them a deal, especially if they acted immediately. This can also take the form of a contractor's telling your parent that they can start the job "tomorrow." Another suspicious variation is when the contractor offers your parent a low price because they want to use the project as a "demonstration."

- Your parent tells you the contractor quoted them a low price at first, but then demanded substantially more money later because of unforeseen expenses, a tactic known as "buying in."

- You notice unplanned physical changes to the interior or exterior of your parent's home or driveway. (Watch out for the infamous driveway resealing or repaving scam. This is when roving bands of crooks work neighborhoods offering to repair driveways for insanely low prices, but use inferior products that wash away in the next rainstorm.)

- Your parent doesn't have a signed estimate or contract with a contractor.

- If your parent has a business card from the contractor, it only has a P.O. box number for an address.

- The contractor didn't present a business license and proof of bonding and insurance.

- The contractor asked for all the money for the job up front, especially if they asked for cash.

- You or a trusted neighbor sees an unfamiliar vehicle (especially an unmarked pickup truck or one with an out-of-state license plate) in front of your parent's house.

- Your parent says the contractor offered or arranged financing for the repairs.
- Your parent tells you the contractor asked them to get building permits for the job.

If any of the signs above are present, it's time to put the steps below into action. Sometimes the scam perpetrators actually cause more damage to a home than they were allegedly trying to repair, therefore it's important to have your parent's home checked right away for possible safety hazards or other issues that could cause even bigger problems.

Checklist for Step 1

_____ Ask your parent if they let the person enter their home, even for a short time. If your parent says yes, consider the possibility of theft and check for missing items including valuables such as money or jewelry as well as credit and debit cards, checks, or other sources of personal information that could be used for identity theft.

_____ Find out how your parent paid for the repairs, both materials and labor. If they paid with a check or credit card, see the steps below.

_____ Ask your parent to show you all the papers they have from the contractor. Gather business cards, invoices, or other documents showing the name and contact information for the contractor.

_____ Ask your parent for any papers regarding a loan to pay for the repairs. If there are any, call an elder law attorney immediately to discuss your options.

_____ Arrange an appointment for a home inspector or consulting engineer to come out and do a thorough check of your parent's home, especially the area(s) affected by the fraudulent work. Consult the American Society for Home Inspectors at www.ashi.org for a referral. You can also get an opinion on structural issues from the National Association of Home Builders at www.nahb.com.

_____ Set up a filing system for all fraud-related material.

_____ Start a master log book of all contacts.

_____ Write down your parent's story about what happened.

_____ Back up all fraud-related computer files weekly.

_____ Start a crime timeline with the information you gather (see Chapter 1).

_____ Consult law enforcement about filing a police report.

_____ Take photos of all work, finished and unfinished.

_____ Call your parent's homeowners insurance company to check on possible coverage for damage.

_____ Check out the price the contractor charged for the work by calling three local reputable contractors and asking for a general price range for what was done. This may be useful information if you suspect the price was unusually high, or if you're not sure what such a repair should have cost. You might need this if you are able to charge the contractor with a crime.

Step 2 for Home Repair Rip-offs

Protect Your Parent: Stop the Bleeding and Lock Down the Assets

There's a high potential for multiple forms of victimization with home repair frauds. Suppose your mom or dad paid the contractor with a check, for example. Now the crook has your parent's account and bank routing numbers, opening up the ugly possibility of further theft. If your parent gave them a credit card to use to buy materials, the con artist can use it to buy extra tools or other items to sell for a profit. Below I've listed a couple of basic steps to address possibilities such as these. See also Chapter 12 on recovering from identity theft for more ideas.

_____ Stop payment on the check if possible, and place a fraud alert on the bank account. It's also a good idea to be sure none of your parent's blank checks are missing.

_____ Call the credit card company that issued the card your parent gave to the contractor to dispute charges and place a fraud alert on the account.

_____ Look for any missing credit or debit cards, personal information, or papers.

_____ Just in case the fraudster took photos of your parent's credit or debit cards, get a copy of their credit reports from each credit reporting agency (www.annualcreditreport.com) and review them. Place a credit freeze or fraud alert with each agency and any other credit card companies involved.

Most of the time a home repair scam will only come to light after the job is over and the fraudster has disappeared. But if you catch the bogus repairs in mid-process, here are some ideas for how to deal with the situation:

_____If your parent was lucky enough to get a contract in writing, according to federal law you should be able to help them cancel the contract if you find out about it within three days of their signing it. Some states allow more time. See the appendix for how to contact your state attorney general for more information, and consult an attorney for help.

_____ Ask the contractor to show you their license, bonding paperwork, and proof of liability insurance and workers compensation insurance. Read any refusal on the contractor's part as a sign to suspend the job immediately.

_____ Call or visit your local police department and tell them what you suspect. Ask if they will send out an officer to help you confront the contractor if they are scheduled to return for more work.

_____ If the contractor is scheduled to come back, call them and delay their return while you research the company or individual and/ or arrange for law enforcement to be there when they arrive.

Step 3 for Home Repair Rip-offs

Recovery; Make Your Recovery Plan

The specifics of your recovery plan will flow from the nature of the work the scam contractor began or completed. Below I list some precautions to take if you have to hire someone else to correct or complete the work, and some helpful resources for more information. I would especially like to recognize the National Center for the Prevention of Home Improvement Fraud's website at www.ncphif.org for these ideas.

_____ Thoroughly check out all contractors you consider for the job of fixing the bogus repairs by calling local references; don't rely on contractor-supplied references alone. Ask for references to customers who are currently doing business with the contractor and those whose work was completed six months or a year ago.

_____ Call your state's attorney general and the Better Business Bureau to check on the contractor. Consider membership in a consumer ratings service such as Angie's List to see what other customers in your area have to say about the contractor. You can also ask personnel at the attorney general's office if your state has a special website for this purpose that you can use, and whether the contractor has been sued by unsatisfied homeowners.

_____ Arrange for written estimates from at least three reputable contractors for correcting the damage or completing unfinished work. Remember that the cheapest estimate is not always the best option!

_____ After choosing a contractor, get a written contract that specifies what work is to be done, start and end dates, material specifications and prices, use of subcontractors, and who's responsible for permits. You may want to include penalties for failure to complete the job in a timely manner. Be sure to get any verbal promises in writing.

_____ Make sure the contractor has up-to-date proof of liability insurance and workers compensation by asking to see their certificates. Their insurance certificate should indicate coverage for property damage and personal liability as well as general liability. Call the contractor's insurance company and verify coverage to ensure it hasn't been canceled since the certificate was issued.

_____ Make sure the contractor meets all bonding and licensing requirements mandated by your parent's city, county, and state.

_____ Ask for a written guarantee or warranty. If the contractor won't provide one, don't do business with them.

_____ Don't pay for the whole job up front. If the contractor wants payment in advance for materials, make the payment directly to the supplier. A general rule is to pay 1/3 at the beginning, 1/3 when the work is half complete, and 1/3 upon finishing. You may also require a mechanic's lien waiver, which protects your parent if the contractor fails to pay others for labor or materials.

_____ Get a lien waiver from the contractor when they complete the work.

_____ Report your parent's victimization to your state's attorney general and the local Better Business Bureau. This may help prevent others from being ripped off and assist law enforcement in prosecuting the criminals.

_____ If you need more specific information about recovery from home repair issues, take a look at nationally syndicated columnist Tim Carter's website at www.askthebuilder.com.

_____ For more good ideas for dealing with contractors before, during, and after a home repair project, see the website for the nonprofit National Center for the Prevention of Home Improvement Fraud at www.ncphif.org.

_____ I have spoken with my parent's tax preparer and informed them about the losses.

_____ I have acquired IRS Publication 547 and have a copy of a police report or attorney general complaint to file with their taxes. (http://www.irs.gov/pub/irs-pdf/p547.pdf)

_____ My parent has had a thorough medical checkup and mental status exam.

_____ I am encouraging and helping my parent enhance their quality of life.

Home repair scams can be costly and upsetting to deal with. Take the necessary steps, perform your due diligence, and make sure the correction gets done right. Always keep reassuring your parent you will get through the nightmare together.

Chapter 12
Recovering from Financial Identity Theft

"Integrity simply means not violating one's own identity."

—Erich Fromm

Who are you, really? Sounds like a question a therapist would ask, doesn't it! But when it comes to identity theft, the question takes on a whole new meaning.

Identity theft (or, more accurately, identity *fraud*) is still the #1 fraud in the US. As I've written elsewhere, many scams involve multiple types of violations. Identity theft in one form or another is part of most of them. When I give talks on identity theft I ask for a show of hands for how many people have been touched in some way by identity theft, either their own or that of a friend, client, or family member. A majority of hands in the room go up.

So what are we talking about here? The US Federal Trade Commission defines it this way: "Identity theft is someone using your personally identifying information, like your name, Social Security number, or credit card number, without your permission, to commit fraud or other crimes." It's essentially someone pretending to be you in order to get goods and services to which they aren't entitled.

There are two ways of understanding identity theft: by the *method* the criminal uses, and by *type* of identity theft based on the criminal's goal for the fraud. Both method and goal are important to understand in helping your parent recover from identity theft.

Two Methods of Committing Identity Theft

The most common methods that identity thieves use are called *synthetic identity theft* and *identity cloning*. Synthetic identity theft is when a thief steals someone's Social Security number and connects it to the name and birthdate of someone else. They are using a real SSN and building a phony or "synthetic" identity around it. For example, they may set up utility or cell phone accounts with the fake identity, followed by a small loan which they repay quickly to build credit in that name. This is followed by a much larger loan which they never repay, but for which the true holder of the SSN may be held responsible.

In identity cloning, which is also known as *identity assumption*, the thief "becomes" the victim. Why do they do this? Sometimes someone steals another's identity for concealment, or to shield them from some reality they don't want to face. More often they will take out credit cards or loans in their victim's name which don't get repaid but which the victim is liable for. What's really scary for elders is that sometimes this involves fraudulent use of health benefits, with potentially harmful consequences for the victim through denial of legitimate care due to policy limits being exceeded. A leading research firm in the field of identity theft, Javelin Strategy and Research, reported there were 1.5 million victims of medical identity theft in 2010.

Major Types of Identity Theft Based on the Criminal's Goal

- Financial identity theft: The perpetrator uses the victim's identity to gain money or goods.

- Criminal identity theft: The perpetrator uses the victim's identity to avoid prosecution for a crime.
- Healthcare or medical identity theft: The perpetrator accesses healthcare by using the victim's identity.
- Social Security identity theft: The perpetrator uses the victim's SSN to gain employment (or other benefits).
- Immigration identity theft: The perpetrator uses the victim's personal information to obtain a "green card" to stay in the USA.

Susceptibility of Elders to Identity Theft

Having your identity stolen, whatever form it takes, can be devastating, costly, and time-consuming to deal with. The elderly are more susceptible to identity theft for several reasons:

- They frequently live alone.
- They tend to be less able to resist high-pressure tactics designed to gain their personal information.
- They often don't use or check their accounts as often as younger people.
- They usually have above-average credit and lots of home equity.
- They are not as naturally security conscious as younger people.
- A computer-savvy older person may not be aware of the sophisticated "phishing" and "spoofing" scams perpetrated via the internet to get their personal information.

When an elderly person realizes they have become a victim of identity theft, they often don't report the crime because they feel ashamed and embarrassed for "allowing" something like that to happen to them. As you work through the recovery process, it is important to make it very clear that there should be no embarrassment associated with being the victim of identity theft. The only embarrassment should be on the part of the individuals who commit such disgusting crimes.

Remember, too, from earlier in this book, how difficult it can be for our elders to recover financially and the role of stress in worsening illnesses, and it's easy to understand how important it is to do everything you can to help your parent recover after having their identity compromised.

A Special Note about Emotional Dynamics

You will likely encounter a frustrating and offensive presumption of guilt in your interactions with people from whom you are seeking help in regard to identity theft. You are trying to prove your parent's innocence to employees who are paid to be suspicious and presume guilt. As Mari Frank writes, "Many people will assume you are making excuses for what you (your impostor) did." It's normal to find this aggravating, but don't take it personally. Go ahead and vent to your spouse, a friend, or another supportive person, but do your best to keep your cool with the employee or other official.

How are you at handling confrontation? This is another difficult dynamic you will probably encounter as you work through the recovery steps for identity theft. Many people are uncomfortable about confrontation in any part of their lives. When the stress is on, as it is with scam recovery, we have a tendency to fall back on old or ingrained ways of functioning (remember, "When we stress, we regress").

The goal for your interactions with suspicious and/or unhelpful people is to *balance firm and kind*. Do not be a pushover, but do not be a bull in a china shop, either. You will most often achieve your aims by treating people with respect, and gently confronting when you must.

Because interacting with bank personnel and others involved in the recovery process can be confusing and cause you to lose your place in the conversation or in your train of thought, take the time and effort to document everything and set up a workable filing system. You may have to refer to something in your documentation at a moment's notice during a phone call, and you'll want to be well prepared to do so. You will help yourself and your parent by being organized, prepared, and collaborative with the employees you deal with. If organizing is hard for you, ask for help from a trustworthy friend or family member.

Focus of This Chapter: Financial Identity Theft

The world of identity theft is especially multi-faceted and complex. As I've written elsewhere, my intent for this chapter is to get you started thinking about recovery while remembering that every situation is different. I have chosen to focus on the high points of recovery from financial identity theft because this type is most likely to affect an elder.

At the end of the checklist for Step 1 below I list the one book I feel you must buy to handle your parent's identity theft problem. Despite the title, Mari J. Frank's book, *The Complete Idiot's Guide to Recovering from Identity Theft*, is absolutely indispensable for its in-depth information and guidance. I want to acknowledge her work as a major resource for this entire chapter. See the appendix for more helpful books and online resources.

Step 1 for Financial Identity Theft

Discovery: Common Signs of Financial Identity Theft

Identity theft (or identity fraud) can lurk in the shadows for some time before coming to light. Here are some signs that indicate identity fraud is occurring:

- Usual bills do not arrive on time, or at all.
- There are unexplained withdrawals, checks, or transfers drawn on your parent's bank and/or credit union accounts.
- Statements or bills come for credit cards or accounts your parent doesn't have.
- Your parent experiences denial of credit or approval of credit at terms not appropriate to their credit history.
- There are calls or letters from financial institutions or collection agencies about unknown purchases or debts.
- There are unauthorized or unknown accounts, loans, charges, or even bankruptcies on your parent's credit report.

In Step 1 your goals are to determine exactly which types of identity theft are present and how bad they are. If you had some idea that your parent had an identity theft problem before you began reading this chapter, I hope you have gained clarity about the type(s) of identity theft affecting your mom or dad. Even though financial identity theft is by far the most common form, keep in mind that there may be more than one type happening simultaneously.

Checklist for Step 1

_____ I or another trusted family member has power of attorney to represent my parent.

_____ I have checked all of my parent's bank, credit union, investment, insurance, and credit card accounts for suspicious activity.

_____ I have determined the types of identity theft likely present in my parent's situation.

_____ I have filed an identity theft report with a local law enforcement agency and with the Federal Trade Commission at 877-ID-THEFT (877-438-4338) or http://www.ftc.gov/

bcp/edu/microsites/idtheft/consumers/filing-a-report.html (remember to keep a copy for your records).

_____ I have obtained copies of my parent's credit reports from all three credit reporting agencies (www.annualcreditreport.com).

_____ I have reviewed my parent's credit reports for fraudulent activity, suspicious accounts (as shown in "soft pulls" and "hard pulls" in the Inquiry Section), and incorrect personal information.

_____ I have contact information and account numbers for all my parent's legitimate accounts.

_____ I have copies of my parent's driver's license, passport, Social Security card, and health insurance card. (Remember to keep these locked up when you're not using them.)

_____ I have a *bank guaranty* of my parent's signature (a document proving the correct appearance of your parent's signature per their bank signature card).

_____ I have gathered contact information about suspicious new accounts by looking up the company name on the credit reports via the internet.

_____ I have ordered and reviewed my parent's complete consumer file from LexisNexis at http://www.lexisnexis.com/risk/ or 800-869-0751. (This may reveal several other types of identity fraud which can be hard to track via credit reports.)

_____ I have checked for fraudulent cell phone or utility accounts through the National Consumer Telecom and Utilities Exchange (NCTUE) at www.nctue.com or 866-343-2821

_____ I have begun a documentation system for phone calls, paper and electronic documents, and fraud-related expenses.

_____ I have set up a master log book (see Chapter 1).

_____ I have started a crime timeline (see Chapter 1).

_____ I am backing up all fraud-related computer files weekly.

_____ I have a copy of *The Complete Idiot's Guide to Recovering from Identity Theft* by Mari J. Frank

Step 2 for Financial Identity Theft

Protect Your Parent: Stop the Bleeding and Lock Down the Assets

In Step 2 you want to end the thieves' unauthorized use of your parent's personal information. This is where you draw the line on further losses.

The following checklist doesn't cover every possible variation, but is intended to help you begin taking the steps relevant to your situation.

Checklist for Step 2

_____ I have placed an initial fraud alert on my parent's credit report with each of the three credit reporting agencies. (You must dispute the fraudulent information on your parent's credit reports immediately after receiving copies of their reports or you will hamper their recovery.)

Equifax:

Page for requesting a fraud alert: https://www.alerts.equifax.com/AutoFraud_Online/jsp/fraudAlert.jsp

888-766-0008

Experian

Page for requesting a fraud alert:

https://www.experian.com/consumer/cac/InvalidateSession.do?code=SECURITYALERT

888-397-3742

TransUnion

To file a fraud alert by email: fvad@transunion.com

800-680-7289

_____ I have called my parent's bank and other financial institutions from Step 1 above to alert them to the presence of identity theft. (Follow up in writing, return receipt requested.)

_____ I have requested a fraud alert with the National Consumer Telecom and Utilities Exchange (NCTUE), if applicable, at www.nctue.com or 866-349-3233.

_____ I have reminded my parent to never pay a bill in their name which was generated through identity theft.

Step 3 for Financial Identity Theft

Recovery: Make Your Recovery Plan

Your particular path to recovery will vary with the specifics of your parent's victimization. Here are some highlights:

_____ I have requested, in writing, an extended fraud alert and/or credit freeze on my parent's credit report with each of the three credit reporting agencies. (Remember to send this and all written correspondence return receipt requested.)

_____ I have closed or formally disputed, in writing, all accounts I know or suspect to be fraudulent. (Remember to ask for the records for each account.)

_____ I have sent a letter to each credit reporting agency disputing fraudulent accounts and requesting that the agency block the incorrect information and provide me with a corrected report. I have submitted a copy of my parent's identity theft report from law enforcement. I requested a credit freeze and included one document to verify my parent's SSN and two documents to verify their address. I made sure the copies are legible.

_____ I have submitted a copy of my parent's identity theft report and a letter requesting removal of the fraudulent accounts and information to each creditor.

_____ I have spoken with my parent's tax preparer and asked them about deducting the recovery-related expenses.

_____ I have made an appointment for a thorough medical checkup and mental status exam for my parent.

_____ I am monitoring my parent's mail.

_____ I am encouraging and helping my parent enhance their quality of life.

Although recovering from identity theft is often complicated, if you take it step by step you will get through it. Use the resources in the appendix for help whenever you need it. Keep going despite the obstacles, and remember your overall mission: restoring your parent's good name.

Final Thoughts and Next Steps

"What we call the beginning is often the end. And to make an end is to make a beginning. The end is where we start from."

—TS Eliot, *Four Quartets*

We have come very far in the journey of scam and fraud recovery. You now have a better idea about how complicated and painful the aftermath can be, but I also hope you feel a greater understanding of intelligent prevention and the possibilities for resilience and a positive recovery. There is no way to completely avoid the pain, and yet I truly wish for you a deeper sense of determination and confidence in your ability to help your parent move on in the best way possible. I genuinely hope *Scammed* has given you useful information, tools, and plans you can customize for your parent and yourself.

I strongly encourage you to practice the prevention ideas in this book and create new ones. I want *Scammed* to inspire a new conversation about scam prevention in the 21st century as our elderly population grows to far exceed historical numbers. I envision a conversation that addresses how to empower elders to build their internal capacity for scam and fraud prevention, while incorporating the unfortunate reality of cognitive impairment into those same prevention efforts. I imagine a strategy for prevention that respects elders' developmental needs for independence and simultaneously protects those who are unable to protect themselves. This is no small feat, but I say let us begin today; the pain from fraud victimization is not going away, and no one should be hurt just because their brain no longer works as well as it used to.

In my frequent talks with elders, I sense in them an eagerness to connect and remain active contributors in life. I hold their wisdom and generosity in very high regard, and treasure the many friends I have made through this work. I wish every elder the peace of mind that comes with knowing how to steer clear of those who would harm them, and I intend for my information to contribute to their experience of that peace.

I also appreciate the multiple ways my friends and colleagues in the fields of mental health, social work, elder law, and eldercare in general support our seniors. I'm privileged to know many good people doing their best to help older adults live better lives and remain vital and active. I am humbled to be your peer.

When Bill's scam came to light, I had no idea it would be the touchstone to an expansion of my own work and mission. I'll never forget the visceral realization that flowed through me that day in July of 2009, about a month after everything blew up; I *knew*, in a very clear and profound way, that this was an enormously important problem facing our society and that I had an opportunity to make a difference, no matter how small it might be. I began this book that day.

I am not so grandiose as to think that I have all the answers. I am, however, delighted to share what I learn in multiple ways with my readers and colleagues. I plan to keep sharing what I find through my website (www.elderlyfraudrecoveryhelp.com), email newsletter, talks, and presentations. The future may hold other avenues and ideas for raising awareness and providing assistance, and I invite you to check my website for updates.

I ask one thing of you: Keep doing all you can to spread the word about scammers and prevent their noxious work from hurting any more of our elders. I am convinced we can all contribute in some way to the worthwhile cause of ensuring our elders' safety.

I'll do my part; I trust you to do yours. Together we can make our world safer for our loved ones and ourselves.

ABOUT THE AUTHOR

A graduate of Texas A & M University and the Brown School of Social Work at Washington University in St. Louis, Art has been in active clinical practice for over ten years. He has been a guest lecturer at Washington University and has conducted trainings for managed behavioral health care companies as well as Fortune 500 corporations. He is especially honored to have been asked to conduct several trauma debriefings with victims of the 9/11 attacks in New York.

Art has also been a speaker on elderly fraud prevention and recovery at both the state and national level. He has trained on topics related to elderly fraud recovery and prevention to professional groups and senior organizations, and has consulted with scam victims' families locally and nationally. He lives in St. Louis with his partner, Frank Krebs, and their chocolate Labrador retriever, Bodie.

About ElderlyFraudRecoveryHelp.com

As Art was helping his stepfather deal with the scam aftermath, he realized he had a unique opportunity to help others who were dealing with a similar challenge. The website www.elderlyfraudrecoveryhelp.com grew out of his desire to provide information and guidance from someone who's "been there."

Beginning with a blog which has had readers from across the world, Art continues to offer a wealth of resources for elder scam recovery and prevention, including his own information and links to helpful websites.

Be sure to visit this site to receive Art's free resources about the ever-changing world of elderly scam prevention and recovery.

APPENDIX

Resources and Recommended Reading

I've found a number of resources that may be helpful to you and your parent, depending on your specific needs. I list them below by type of resource and by type of scam or fraud. Some resources appear in more than one category.

This is the kind of help I wished for when I started helping Bill, so I hope you find it useful.

US Federal Government Resources

Website for the US Agency on Aging's Eldercare Locator, through which you can access the local number for Adult Protective Services for your area
http://www.eldercare.gov
800-677-1116

Website for the US Federal Trade Commission, which has a great deal of general information about frauds and scams against the elderly
http://www.ftc.gov

Website to use for finding your local US Secret Service field office, which has jurisdiction over money wired overseas from frauds and scams
http://www.secretservice.gov/field_offices.shtml

Website for the Federal Bureau of Investigation (FBI) Internet Crime Complaint Center
http://www.ic3.gov/default.aspx

General Information about Scams and Scam Recovery

There are many websites that provide information about scams and scam recovery. Here are some of the better ones I've found:

AARP
http://www.aarp.org

Better Business Bureau
http://www.bbb.com

Clark Howard, a nationally syndicated consumer reporter and advocate (Note: Click on the tab for "Clark's topics," then click on either "consumer issues/id theft" or "scams and rip-offs," depending on what you're looking for.)
http://www.clarkhoward.com/

Consumer Federation of America
http://www.consumerfed.org

Crimes of Persuasion (arguably the most complete information site on the internet about frauds and scams in general)
http://www.crimes-of-persuasion.com

Detective Joe Roubicek's website on exploitation of the elderly
http://www.exploitationelderly.com

FBI page on Scams Against Elders
http://www.fbi.gov/scams-safety/fraud/seniors/seniors

Fraud Aid, a not-for-profit organization with an emphasis on fraud victim advocacy and support
http://www.fraudaid.com

Frauds and Scams (mainly a resource for private investigators, but has some useful information for laypeople)
http://www.fraudsandscams.com

Appendix

National Consumer League
http://www.nclnet.org
http://www.fraud.org
http://www.fakechecks.org

Identity Theft

Identity Theft Prevention and Survival, the website for Mari Frank, an attorney specializing in identity theft and the author of my top-rated book for handling identity theft, *The Complete Idiot's Guide to Recovering from Identity Theft*
http://www.identitytheft.org

Identity Theft Resource Center
http://www.idtheftcenter.org

Privacy Rights Clearinghouse
http://www.privacyrights.org

US Federal Trade Commission
http://www.ftc.gov/bcp/edu/microsites/idtheft/

Most states have helpful resources concerning identity theft on their state attorney general's website as well. See the section later in this appendix.

Relevant Websites for Each Step of the 3-Step Process

Step 1—Discovery: Gather the Vital Information Quickly

While most of your work in this step will be done at your parent's home through asking your parent questions, you may have to do some additional detective work, especially if your parent is in denial about what's really happening. Here's a link to an area code map for Canada, useful because many telemarketing scammers targeting American seniors call from British Columbia and other Canadian provinces:
http://www.canada411.ca/search/areaCode.html

Here's a link to an area code map for the Caribbean (another source of many scam calls targeting American seniors, especially Jamaica—area code 876):
http://www.lincmad.com/caribmap.html

Crimes of Persuasion offers a lot of good, general information about types of scams, which may help you understand exactly what is happening.
http://www.crimes-of-persuasion.com

(Also see "General Information about Scams and Scam Recovery" above.)

Step 2—Protect Your Parent: Stop the Bleeding and Lock Down the Assets

National Academy of Elder Law Attorneys
http://www.naela.org
703-942-5711

Credit Reporting Agencies

If a person files a fraud alert with one agency, they typically notify the other two. Nevertheless, I've included contact information for all three below.

Equifax
Page for requesting a fraud alert: https://www.alerts.equifax.com/AutoFraud_Online/jsp/fraudAlert.jsp
800-525-6285

Experian
Page for requesting a fraud alert:
https://www.experian.com/consumer/cac/InvalidateSession.do?code=SECURITYALERT
888-397-3742

Appendix

TransUnion
To file a fraud alert by email: fvad@transunion.com
800-680-7289

To get a copy of your parent's credit report:
www.annualcreditreport.com or 877-322-8228

Major Credit Card Companies:

American Express
http://www.americanexpress.com
800-528-4800

Discover
http://www.discovercard.com
800-347-2683

MasterCard
http://www.mastercard.us
800-627-8372

Visa
http://www.visa.com
800-847-2911

Step 3—Recovery: Plan Your Parent's Financial Recovery

Financial advisors to assess the damage and develop a cash management or rebuilding plan:

The Garrett Planning Network
www.garrettplanningnetwork.com

National Association of Personal Financial Advisors
(www.napfa.org)

Scammed

US Internal Revenue Service Publication 547, Casualties, Disasters, and Thefts (how to handle deducting losses on taxes from scam- and fraud-related theft)
http://www.irs.gov/pub/irs-pdf/p547.pdf

Emotional Recovery (resources for elders and their family members)

American Association for Geriatric Psychiatry
http://www.aagponline.org

American Association for Marriage and Family Therapy
http://www.aamft.org

American Association of Pastoral Counselors
http://www.aapc.org

American Counseling Association
http://www.counseling.org

American Mental Health Counselors Association
http://www.amhca.org

American Psychological Association
http://www.apa.org

National Association of Social Workers
http://www.socialworkers.org

National Coalition on Mental Health and Aging
http://www.ncmha.org

National Center for Victims of Crime
http://www.ncvc.org

National Organization for Victim Assistance (NOVA)
http://www.trynova.org

Appendix

Link to the Eight-Item Informant Interview to Differentiate Aging and Dementia® (AD8)
http://alzheimer.wustl.edu/About_Us/PDFs/AD8form2005.pdf

BOOKS

Some books appear in more than one category because they provide useful guidance in multiple areas. All are available for purchase through Amazon.

Scams and Frauds

These titles provide a good overview of the huge variety of frauds and scams happening to our parents:

Crimes of Persuasion by Les Henderson

Fleecing Grandma and Grandpa by Betty L. Alt and Sandra K. Wells

Scambusters! by Ron Smith

The Truth about Avoiding Scams by Steve Weisman

Exploitation of the Elderly

Financial Abuse of the Elderly: A Detective's Case Files of Exploitation Crimes by Joe Roubicek

Is Your Parent in Good Hands? Protecting Your Aging Parent from Financial Abuse and Neglect by Edward J. Carnot, Esq.

Preventing Scams and Frauds

Is Your Parent in Good Hands? Protecting Your Aging Parent from Financial Abuse and Neglect by Edward J. Carnot, Esq.

Fleecing Grandma and Grandpa by Betty L. Alt and Susan K. Wells

Scammed

Scam-proof Your Life by Sid Kirchheimer

Scambusters! by Ron Smith

The Truth about Avoiding Scams by Steve Weisman

Scammers and the Psychology of Scamming

In Sheep's Clothing by Dr. George K. Simon

Without Conscience, by Dr. Robert Hare

The Sociopath Next Door by Dr. Martha Stout

The Psychopath: Emotion and the Brain by James Blair, Derek Mitchell, and Karina Blair

Unmasking the Psychopath: Antisocial Personality and Related Symptoms (multiple authors, from Norton Professional Books)

Effectively Communicating with Elders

Are Your Parents Driving You Crazy? By Joseph A. Ilardo

Coping with Your Difficult Older Parent by Grace Lebow and Barbara Kane

Elder Rage, Or…Take My Father, Please! By Jacqueline Marcell

How to Communicate with Alzheimer's: A Practical Guide and Workbook for Families by Susan Koehler

How to Say it to Seniors by David Solie

Handling Family Issues

Caring for Yourself While Caring for Your Aging Parents by Claire Berman

Appendix

Self-care

Caring for Yourself While Caring for Your Aging Parents by Claire Berman

Chicken Soup for the Caregiver's Soul by Jack Canfield

50 Ways to Soothe Yourself without Food by Dr. Susan Albers

Self-Care for Caregivers: A Twelve Step Approach by Pat Samples

Taking Care of Me: The Habits of Happiness by Mary Kay Mueller

Taking Care of Parents Who Didn't Take Care of You: Making Peace with Aging Parents by Eleanor Cade

The Emotional Survival Guide for Caregivers—Looking after Yourself and Your Family While Helping an Aging Parent by Dr. Barry J. Jacobs

Interventions and Dealing with Denial

Face It and Fix It by Ken Seeley

How to Say It to Seniors by David Solie

Love First: A Family's Guide to Intervention by Debra Jay

Identity Theft

How to Survive Identity Theft: Regain Your Money, Credit, and Reputation by David H. Holtzman

Identity Theft: How to Protect Your Most Valuable Asset by Robert Hammond

Stopping Identity Theft: 10 Easy Steps to Security by Scott Mitic

The Complete Idiot's Guide to Recovering from Identity Theft by Mari J. Frank (especially good despite the title)

The Official Identity Theft Prevention Handbook by Denis G. Kelly

The Truth about Identity Theft by Jim Stickley

The Wall Street Journal Complete Identity Theft Guidebook by Terri Cullen

Listing of State Attorneys Generals' Contact Information

I've included here resource listings for relevant scam and fraud situations. Please be sure to click on the link below for your state's attorney general as well. Most states have helpful resources on their websites.

National Association of Attorneys General
http://www.naag.org/

Alabama
http://www.ago.state.al.us/
Consumer Hotline: 800-392-5658 or 334-242-7334
Victim Assistance Hotline: 800-626-7676 or 334-242-7342

Alaska
http://www.law.state.ak.us/
Webpage for filing a complaint: http://www.law.state.ak.us/department/civil/consumer/cp_complaint.html

Arizona
http://www.azag.gov/

For more information Contact:
Crime, Fraud & Victim Resource Center

Appendix

Arizona Attorney General's Office
1275 West Washington Street
Phoenix, Arizona 85007
602.542.2123   602.542.2123   (Phoenix)
520.628.6504   520.628.6504   (Tucson)
800.352.8431   800.352.8431   (toll free in State of Arizona, outside Maricopa and Pima Counties)
602.364.1970 (fax)
communityservices@azag.gov

Arkansas
http://www.arkansasag.gov/
For consumer complaints: http://www.arkansasag.gov/consumers_consumer_complaints.html

California
http://oag.ca.gov/
For consumer complaints: http://ag.ca.gov/consumers/general.php

Colorado
http://www.coloradoattorneygeneral.gov/
For consumer complaints: https://www.coloradoattorneygeneral.gov/departments/consumer_protection/file_consumer_complaint

Connecticut
http://www.ct.gov/ag/site/default.asp
Complaint form: http://www.ct.gov/ag/lib/ag/consumers/consumercomplaintform032011.pdf

Delaware
http://attorneygeneral.delaware.gov/
complaint form: http://www.attorneygeneral.delaware.gov/media/pdf/complaintform.pdf
Phone: (302) 577-8600 or (800) 220-5424

District of Columbia
http://oag.dc.gov/DC/OAG

complaint form:
http://government.dc.gov/DC/Government/
Data+&+Transparency/Consumer+Protection/
Submit+Consumer+Complaints/Consumer+Complaint+Form
Consumer Protection Hotline (202) 442-9828

Florida
http://myfloridalegal.com/

complaint form:
http://myfloridalegal.com/Contact.nsf/Contact?OpenForm&Secti
on=Economic_Crimes
Telephone: (850) 414-3990
Toll Free within Florida: 1-866-966-7226

Georgia

(Note: Georgia is one of three states in the US in which the attorney
general does not bear responsibility for investigating consumer fraud.
The responsibility for investigating consumer complaints in Georgia
rests with the Governor's Office of Consumer Affairs.)
http://consumer.georgia.gov/

complaint form:
http://consumer.georgia.gov/pdf/Complaintform.pdf
PHONE: 404-651-8600 (ATLANTA)
FAX: 404-651-9018
TOLL-FREE IN GA OUTSIDE METRO ATLANTA:
800-869-1123

Hawaii
http://hawaii.gov/ag/
Department of the Attorney General

425 Queen Street
Honolulu, HI 96813 (Map)
Telephone: (808) 586-1500
Fax: (80]8) 586-1239

Elder Abuse Justice Unit
Office of the Prosecuting Attorney
1060 Richards Street
Honolulu, Hawaii 96813
(808) 768-6452

Idaho
http://www.ag.idaho.gov/index.html

consumer complaints:
http://www.ag.idaho.gov/consumerProtection/forms/
ConsumerForm_Online.pdf
954 W. Jefferson, 2nd Floor
P.O. Box 83720
Boise, ID 83720-0010
Phone (208) 334-2424
Fax (208) 334-4151

Illinois
http://illinoisattorneygeneral.gov/

consumer complaints:
http://illinoisattorneygeneral.gov/consumers/conscomp.pdf
Illinois Attorney General
Consumer Fraud Bureau
500 South Second Street
Springfield, IL 62706
217-782-1090
1-800-243-0618 (Toll free in IL)
TTY: 1-877-844-5461

Indiana
http://www.in.gov/attorneygeneral/

Comprehensive website for Indiana consumer issues:
http://www.indianaconsumer.com

printable complaint form:
http://www.in.gov/core/faqs.html?faqid=1391&p_created=1261505117

Consumer Protection Division
Office of the Indiana Attorney General
302 W. Washington St., 5th Floor
Indianapolis, IN 46204

You can also request a complaint form by calling 1.800.382.5516 or 317.232.6330.

Iowa
http://www.iowaattorneygeneral.org/

to file a complaint online ONLY:
http://www.state.ia.us/government/ag/file_complaint/online_2.html

printable/mailable version of complaint form:
http://www.state.ia.us/government/ag/images/pdfs/ConsumerProtectionComplaintForm.pdf

Tom Miller
Consumer Protection Division
Attorney General of Iowa
Hoover State Office Building
1300 E. Walnut, Des Moines, Iowa 50319
515-281-5926
E-mail: consumer@ag.state.ia.us

Appendix

Kansas
http://www.ksag.org/

to file a complaint:
http://www.ksag.org/page/file-a-complaint
fax number: (785) 291-3699
Elder abuse page: http://www.ksag.org/page/elder-abuse

Kentucky
http://ag.ky.gov/

to file a complaint:
http://ag.ky.gov/civil/consumerprotection/complaints/forms.htm
Consumer Protection Division (502) 696-5389
Consumer Protection Division
1024 Capital Center Drive
Frankfort, KY 40601

Louisiana
http://www.ag.louisiana.gov/

to file a complaint:
http://www.ag.louisiana.gov/Complaint.aspx?articleID=16&catID=15
Consumer info line (if a victim of elder fraud) 1-800-351-4889

Maine
http://www.maine.gov/ag/

to file a complaint: http://www.maine.gov/ag/consumer/
complaints/complaint_form.shtml

Attorney General's Consumer
Information and Mediation Service
6 State House Station
Augusta, Maine 04333
207-626-8849 or toll-free at 1-800-436-2131
Email: consumer.mediation@maine.gov

Maryland
http://www.oag.state.md.us/

to file a complaint:
http://www.oag.state.md.us/Consumer/complaint.htm
Consumer Protection Division
Consumer hotline:
(410) 528-8662
Mon-Fri 9 am-3 pm

Massachusetts
http://www.mass.gov/?pageID=cagohomepage&L=1&L0=Home&sid=Cago

to file a complaint:
https://www.eform.ago.state.ma.us/ago_eforms/forms/piac_ecomplaint.action

Office of the Attorney General
Public Inquiry & Assistance Center (PIAC)
One Ashburton Place
Boston, MA 02108

Elder Hotline (888) 243-5337

Michigan
http://www.michigan.gov/ag/

to file a complaint:
https://secure.ag.state.mi.us/complaints/consumer.aspx

Consumer Protection Division
P.O. Box 30213
Lansing, MI 48909-7713
Consumer Protection Division: (517) 373-1140 or
toll free 1-877-765-8388

Minnesota
http://www.ag.state.mn.us/

to file a complaint:
http://www.ag.state.mn.us/Consumer/Complaint.asp

Office of Minnesota Attorney General Lori Swanson
1400 Bremer Tower
445 Minnesota Street
St. Paul, MN 55101
(651) 296-3353
1-800-657-3787
TTY: (651) 297-7206
TTY: 1-800-366-4812

Mississippi
http://www.ago.state.ms.us/

to file a complaint:
http://www.ago.state.ms.us/images/uploads/forms/MSAGO_
Complaint_Form.pdf

Consumer Protection Division
Office of the Attorney General
P.O. Box 22947
Jackson, Mississippi 39225-2947
(601) 359-4230 or in Mississippi 1-800-281-4418
Fax (601) 359-4231

Missouri
http://ago.mo.gov/

for consumer complaints:
http://ago.mo.gov/consumercomplaint.htm

Consumer Hotline: (800) 392-8222

Montana

http://www.doj.mt.gov/

to file a complaint:
http://www.doj.mt.gov/consumer/consumer/forms.
asp#consumercomplaints

DEPARTMENT OF JUSTICE

Office of Consumer Protection
2225 11th Avenue
PO BOX 200151
Helena, MT 59620-0151
Phone: (406) 444-4500
1-800-481-6896

Nebraska

http://www.ago.state.ne.us/

To file a complaint:
http://www.ago.state.ne.us/consumer/emailforms/consumer_
complaint.htm

Consumer Protection Hotline: (800) 727-6432
Consumer Protection Hotline: En Espanol (888) 850-7555
Fax: (402) 471-0006
Senior Outreach Hotline: (888) 287-0778

Nevada

http://ag.state.nv.us/

To file a complaint:
http://ag.state.nv.us/complaints/complaints.htm

Hotlines for fraud, Medicare fraud, and identity theft:
http://ag.state.nv.us/about/hotlines/hotlines.htm

Nevada Division of Aging Services, Elder Protective Services
775-688-2964
(after-hours through the Crisis Call Center at 800-992-5757)

New Hampshire
http://doj.nh.gov/

To file a complaint:
http://www.egov.nh.gov/consumercomplaint/

OFFICE OF THE ATTORNEY GENERAL
CONSUMER PROTECTION AND ANTITRUST BUREAU
33 CAPITOL STREET
CONCORD, NEW HAMPSHIRE 03301
Tel.: (603) 271-3641
Fax: (603) 223-6202

New Jersey
http://www.state.nj.us/oag/

To file a complaint:
http://www.nj.gov/oag/ca/comp.htm

Newark Consumer Service Center
P.O. Box 45025
Newark, New Jersey 07101
973-504-6200

New Mexico
http://www.nmag.gov/

To file a complaint:
http://www.nmag.gov/office/Divisions/CP/complaint.aspx

To report a scam:
http://www.nmag.gov/articles/scamalerts.aspx
Consumer Protection Division: 800-678-1508

New York
http://www.ag.ny.gov/

To file a complaint:
http://www.ag.ny.gov/bureaus/consumer_frauds/filing_a_consumer_complaint.html

Consumer Helpline: 1-800-771-7755

North Carolina
http://www.ncdoj.gov/

To file a complaint:
http://www.ncdoj.gov/Consumer/2-2-12-File-a-Complaint.aspx
toll free within North Carolina: 1-877-5-NO-SCAM
(919) 716-6000 from outside of North Carolina
(919) 716-0058 for Spanish speakers.

North Dakota
http://www.ag.state.nd.us/

To file a complaint:
http://www.ag.state.nd.us/CPAT/PDFFiles/SFN7418.pdf

Consumer Protection
1-800-472-2600 within ND only

Ohio
http://www.ohioattorneygeneral.gov/

To file a complaint:
http://www.ohioattorneygeneral.gov/ConsumerComplaint

Help Center
Toll-free: 800-282-0515
Local: 614-466-4986
Monday - Friday 8 a.m. - 7 p.m.

Oklahoma
http://www.oag.state.ok.us/

To file a complaint:
http://www.oag.state.ok.us/oagweb.nsf/complaint.html

OKC 405-521-3921
Tulsa 918-581-2885

Oregon
http://www.doj.state.or.us/

To file a complaint:
http://www.doj.state.or.us/finfraud/engexplanation.shtml(English)
http://www.doj.state.or.us/finfraud/spexplanation.shtml (Spanish)

503-378-4320 from Salem
503-229-5576 from Portland (toll free)
1-877-877-9392 elsewhere in Oregon (toll free)
email: consumer.hotline@doj.state.or.us
fax: (503) 378-5017

Pennsylvania
http://www.attorneygeneral.gov/

To file a complaint:
http://www.attorneygeneral.gov/Complaints.aspx

1-800-441-2555 - Bureau of Consumer Protection
1-866-623-2137 - Elder Abuse Unit

Rhode Island
http://www.riag.state.ri.us/

To file a complaint:
http://www.riag.state.ri.us/documents/consumer/
ConsumerComplaintForm.pdf
General Helpline: (401) 274-4400

South Carolina
http://www.scag.gov/

To file a complaint:
http://www.scconsumer.gov/dcacf/dcapolicy.htm

South Carolina Department of Consumer Affairs
Phone (803) 734-4200
Fax: (803) 734-4286
1-800-922-1594 (Toll free within S.C.)

South Dakota
http://atg.sd.gov/

To file a complaint:
http://atg.sd.gov/Consumers/HandlingComplaints/
ConsumerComplaintForm.aspx

Division of Consumer Protection
1302 E Hwy 14
Suite 3
Pierre SD 57501-8503

Phone: (605) 773-4400
Consumer Help Line: 1-800-300-1986 (South Dakota only)
Fax: 773-7163
E-Mail: consumerhelp@state.sd.us

Tennessee
http://www.tn.gov/attorneygeneral/

To file a complaint:
http://www.tn.gov/attorneygeneral/cpro/filecomplaint.html

Tennessee Division of Consumer Affairs
500 James Robertson Pkwy., 5th Floor
Nashville, TN 37243-0600

Telephone: (615) 741-4737
Fax: (615) 532-4994
If Inside Tennessee: (800) 342-8385

Texas
https://www.oag.state.tx.us/

To file a complaint:
https://www.oag.state.tx.us/consumer/complain.shtml

(800) 252-8011

Utah
http://attorneygeneral.utah.gov/my_mission.html

To file a complaint:
http://consumerprotection.utah.gov/complaints/index.html

General Office Numbers:
(801) 366-0260, (801) 538-9600, (801) 366-0300
Toll Free within the State of Utah: (800) AG4 INFO (244-4636)
E-Mail: uag@utah.gov

Vermont
http://www.atg.state.vt.us/

To file a complaint:
http://www.uvm.edu/consumer/?Page=complaint.html

Consumer Assistance: Toll Free In VT (800)649-2424 or (802) 656-3183

E-mail: consumer@uvm.edu
Consumer Assistance Program
146 University Place
Burlington, VT 05405
FAX: (802) 656-1423

Virginia
http://www.oag.state.va.us/

To file a complaint:
http://www.vdacs.virginia.gov/forms-pdf/cp/oca/complaint/oca1complaint.pdf

Consumer Protection Hotline: (800) 552-9963 if calling from Virginia, or (804) 786-2042 if calling from the Richmond area or from outside Virginia.

Washington
http://www.atg.wa.gov/

To file a complaint:
http://www.atg.wa.gov/FileAComplaint.aspx

1-800-551-4636 (in Washington only)
206-464-6684
1-800-833-6384 for the hearing impaired

West Virginia
http://www.wvago.gov/

To file a complaint:
http://www.wvago.gov/takeaction.cfm

Consumer Hotline: 1-800-368-8808

Wisconsin
http://www.doj.state.wi.us/

To file a complaint:
http://www.doj.state.wi.us/dls/ConsProt/cp_complaints.asp

Consumer Hotline: (800) 422-7128; (608) 224-4953

Wyoming
http://attorneygeneral.state.wy.us/

To file a complaint:
http://attorneygeneral.state.wy.us/PDF/Complaintform.pdf

Attorney General's Office
123 Capitol Building
200 W. 24th Street
Cheyenne, WY 82002
(307) 777-7841
(307) 777-6869 FAX
(307) 777-5351 TDD